Diverse yet United

Diverse yet United

Communicating Truth in Charity

POPE FRANCIS

WITH A FOREWORD BY KEVIN RHOADES,
BISHOP OF FORT WAYNE-SOUTH BEND,
AND A PREFACE BY JUSTIN WELBY, ARCHBISHOP OF CANTERBURY
WITH THE COLLABORATION OF NICOLE PAGLIA

Our Sunday Visitor
Huntington, Indiana

Published in English by Our Sunday Visitor Publishing Division, Our
Sunday Visitor, Inc., 200 Noll Plaza, Huntington, IN 46750; 1-800-348-
2440; www.osv.com.

ISBN: 978-1-68192-740-4 (Inventory No. T2613)
eISBN: 978-1-68192-741-1
LCCN: 2021937202

Cover and interior design: Lindsey Riesen
Cover art: Adobe Stock

PRINTED IN THE UNITED STATES OF AMERICA

TABLE OF CONTENTS

• • •

FOREWORD

Veritas in caritate; Caritas in veritate: "Truth in charity; Charity in truth" (see Eph 4:15). These Pauline phrases, as Pope Benedict XVI pointed out, complement and fulfill each other. Further, they cannot, by their very nature, be competitive: Truth is no impediment to charity; charity is no threat to truth. Unfortunately, our contemporary world, and even the Church, is experiencing a deep polarization in which genuine conversation and fruitful dialogue are more and more difficult to attain. Differences of perspective or viewpoint and good-faith disagreements, sometimes over difficult, important, and highly sensitive questions, are rapidly personalized, and opponents, rather than engaging in rational, charitable discourse — a discourse rooted in truth and love — and participants all too quickly demonize each another.

During his pontificate, the Holy Father, Pope Francis, has encouraged us all to avoid the pitfalls of both a "cancel culture" and a harsh, insensitive rigidity. As Catholics, we should have a robust confidence in the truth and at the same time operate always out of a deep charity that seeks the good of the other. A genuine openness to others does not necessarily entail an abandonment of principles, nor does the recognition of objective — and revealed — truth imply a smug superiority. "To whom much is given, much is required" (see Lk 12:48), and we who have been graced recipients of the gifts of faith, hope, and charity are called to live and to relate to others precisely from within these theological virtues.

In this collection of texts, the reader will discover the pope speaking to all of us about relationship: our relationship with the Lord and, more, how that primary relationship affects our relationships with others. Taken from various moments in a very active pontificate, these texts offer us considerable food for thought as we reflect on the network of relationships which comprise our life: Do we relate to others as competitors? Do we see others as persons rather than as objects of our frustration or resentment? How do we speak to and about the various persons God in his providence has placed in our life? Is our love and defense of the truth clothed in charity? Do we allow Christian charity to be reduced simply to the level of emotion and feeling? Are we more concerned with "winning" an argument, or in leading others to friendship with Jesus? In our pursuit of the truth in charity, do we place greater emphasis on our own efforts and abilities than on the overarching providence of God and his grace? Thoughtful readers will ask themselves these and many other questions as they ponder the words of the Holy Father.

Living the truth in charity is not a science but an art, one requiring much grace, and remains a delicate balancing act as we navigate the tensions between this age and the age to come. May we all be found good and faithful servants of the truth in charity.

Most Reverend Kevin C. Rhoades, DD, JCL, STL
Bishop of the Diocese of Fort Wayne-South Bend

PREFACE

We, who are many, are one body in Christ, and
individually we are members one of another.
— Romans 12:5
God saw everything that he had made,
and indeed, it was very good.
— Genesis 1:31

God created human beings in his image, and yet human
beings are varied and diverse. In their variety and diversity
each is, nevertheless, made in God's image and loved by God.
God looks at all that he has made, and he sees that what he
has made is very good.

When God looks at the world, and at the people in it, he

13

looks with eyes of love. In this volume, *Diverse yet United*, we read the reflections of the Holy Father on human relationships: relationships between people made in the image of God. So often human relationships are fraught with difficulty leading to separation. This is because human beings, though made in God's image, are fallible and fallen, and in our sin we lose the ability to look at one another with the perfect love with which God looks on us. In relationships we can be at our best, but we can also be at our worst.

My brother in Christ, Pope Francis, lays before us in his words the promise of divine love and mercy: the love that God has for his people and the invitation that God gives to each of us to be in a relationship with him.

The best and most fruitful human relationships are those which are built on the love that God has for us. In his reflection on the story of the rich young man, Pope Francis reminds us that when Jesus looked at the rich man, he loved him. St. John Henry Newman, as the pope notes, reflected that the arguments we wage with one another are as much about our disposition to each other than about the merits of the case we are arguing. If we can look on another with love, as Jesus looked on the rich young man, then our relationship with the other person will be all the richer. If we first apologize, we are able to forgive; if we first listen, we are able all the better to speak.

And the breakdown of human relationships through sin, hunger for power, and the inability or unwillingness to love, to listen, to apologize, and to forgive often spills over into a breakdown in relationships between groups of people and between nations. The result of this can be catastrophic, as human history shows through such tragedies as war and forced migration.

In their joint declaration [in Jerusalem in 2014] Pope Francis and the Ecumenical Patriarch, His All Holiness Bartholomew I, stated, "We are deeply convinced that not weapons, but dialogue, forgiveness and reconciliation are the only possible means of achieving peace." *[Siamo profondamente convinti che non le armi, ma il dialogo, il perdono e la riconciliazione sono gli unici strumenti possibili per conseguire la pace.]* But, as human beings made in the image of God, we are bound together in a relationship with one another. It is incumbent on every one of us to work for reconciliation between people, and for reconciliation between human beings and God.

I am profoundly grateful for my friendship with Pope Francis and for the commitment that we share to the ministry of reconciliation. There is a great deal to learn from his words and writings contained in this book.

May the grace of the Lord Jesus Christ, and the love of God, and the koinonia of the Holy Spirit be with you all (see 2 Cor 13:14).

Justin Welby, Archbishop of Canterbury
Church of England

SOME WORDS ABOUT RELATIONSHIPS

God[1] is not solitude, but communion. He is love, and therefore communication, because love always communicates, indeed it communicates itself in order to encounter the other. ... We Christians are called to manifest that communion which marks our identity as believers. Faith itself, in fact, is a relationship, an encounter; and under the impulse of God's love we can communicate, welcome, and understand the gift of the other and respond in kind.

The[2] Gospel has the power to change our lives! Do not forget this. That is the Good News, which transforms us only when we let ourselves be transformed by it. That is why I always ask you to have daily contact with the Gospel, to read it every day, a passage, a passage to meditate on it and to take it with you everywhere: in your pocket, in your bag. ... That is, to nourish yourselves every day with this inexhaustible source of salvation. Do not forget! Read a passage from the Gospel every day. It is the power that changes us, that transforms us: It changes our lives, it changes our hearts.

Jesus[3] speaks of the great love of the owner of a vineyard, the symbol of God's people. He has called us with love; he watches over us. But then he gives us freedom; he "loans" us all this love. It is as if he were saying to us, "Guard and care for my love as I care for you." This is the dialogue between God and us: caring for love. Everything begins with this love.

The[4] Holy Spirit urges us to go out of ourselves to go toward others!

If[5] you do not pray, if you do not talk to Jesus, you do not know him.

Prayer[6] disarms incomprehension and generates dialogue where there is open conflict. If it is sincere and persevering, it will make our voice gentle and firm, capable of being heard even by the leaders of nations.

The communication[7] of the Faith can only be done through witnessing, and this is love. Not with our ideas, but with the Gospel lived in our own existence, which the Holy Spirit enlivens within us. It is like a synergy between us and the Holy Spirit, and this leads to witness. The Church is carried forward by the saints, precisely those who give this witness.

Faith[8], which is like a seed in the depths of the heart, blossoms when we allow ourselves to be "drawn" by the Father to Jesus, and we "go to Him" with an open heart, without prejudice. We then recognize in his face the Face of God, and in his words the Word of God, because the Holy Spirit has made us enter into the relationship of love and life that exists between Jesus and God the Father. And there we receive the gift: the gift of faith.

Life[9] exists where there are bonds, communion, brotherhood. And it is a life stronger than death when it is built on true relationships and bonds of faithfulness. On the other hand, there is no life where we pretend to belong only to ourselves and to live as an island. In these attitudes death prevails. It is selfishness. If I live for myself, I am sowing death in my own heart.

The[10] language of truth and love is the universal language: Even illiterate people can understand it. Everyone understands the language of truth and love. If you go forth with the truth of your heart, with sincerity and with love, everyone will understand you — even if you cannot speak, but can only offer a caress, so long as it is truthful and loving.

An[11] authentic dialogue is always a meeting between persons with a name, a face, a story, and not only an exchange of ideas.

There are[12] so many human issues to discuss and share. In dialogue it is always possible to come closer to the truth, which is God's gift, and to enrich one another. To dialogue means to be convinced that the other has something good to say, to make room for the other's point of view, opinion, proposals, without falling — obviously — into relativism. And in order to have a dialogue, we need to lower our defenses and open our doors.

In[13] your family, do you know how to communicate? Or

are you like those kids at the table, each with a cell phone, texting? At that table there seems to be a silence as if they were at Mass. ... But they are not communicating with each other. We need to resume dialogue in the family: Fathers, parents, children, grandparents, and siblings need to communicate with one another.

How[14] easy it is, though, to let ourselves be carried away by a common opinion, by a defeatism, by a pessimism that paralyzes and blinds us! "By force of habit we no longer stand up to evil. We 'let things be,' or as others have decided they ought to be" (*Gaudete et Exsultate*, 137). Let us ask for *parresia*, for the frankness that comes from the Holy Spirit and that helps us to trust in the truth of Christ that sets us free. Let us go beyond the wall of sadness and resignation and let us help people to open their eyes and ears, and above all their hearts, to be caretakers of one another and to realize that they are sons and daughters of the one Father.

OUR FAITH IN THE GOD OF RELATIONSHIPS

GOD IS LOVE

The[1] Trinity is the communion of Divine Persons who are one with the others, one for the others, one in the others: This communion is the life of God, the mystery of the love of the Living God. Jesus revealed this mystery to us. He spoke to us of God as the Father; he spoke to us of the Spirit; and he spoke to us of himself as the Son of God. Thus he revealed this mystery to us. After he rose, he sent the disciples to evangelize to the peoples. He told them to baptize them "in the name of the Father and of the Son and of the Holy Spirit" (Mt 28:19). This command is entrusted by Christ in all ages to the Church, which has inherited the missionary mandate from the apostles. He also directs it to each one of us who, through the power of baptism, are part of his community.

Therefore, today's liturgical solemnity, while making us contemplate the amazing mystery from which we come and toward which we are going, renews for us the mission of living in communion with God and living in communion among ourselves on the model of the divine communion. We are called to live not as one without the others, above or against the others, but one with the others, for the others, and in the others. This means to accept and witness in harmony the beauty of the Gospel, experiencing love for one another and for all, sharing joy and suffering, learning to ask for and grant forgiveness, appreciating various charisms under the guidance of pastors. In a word, we have been entrusted with the task of edifying ecclesial communities which increasingly become families, capable of reflecting the splendor of the Trinity, and evangelizing not only with the words, but with the power of the love of God that lives within us.

The Trinity, as I said, is also the ultimate goal toward which our earthly pilgrimage is directed. The journey of Christian life is indeed essentially a "Trinitarian" journey: The Holy Spirit guides us to full knowledge of Christ's teachings and reminds us what Jesus taught us. Jesus, in turn, came into the world to make the Father known to us, to guide us to him, to reconcile us with him. Everything in Christian life revolves around the Mystery of the Trinity and is fulfilled according to this infinite mystery. Therefore, we seek to always hold high the "tone" of our life, remembering what goal, what glory we exist for, work for, struggle for, suffer for — and what immense reward we are called to. This mystery embraces our entire life and our entire Christian being. We remember it, for example, each time we make the Sign of the Cross: in the name of the Father, of the Son, and of the Holy Spirit. And now I invite you, all together, and out loud, to make this Sign of the Cross: "In the name of the Father, and of the Son, and of the Holy Spirit!"

GOD LOVES TO COMMUNICATE HIMSELF

God's desire[2] (is) to communicate himself, in what theologians call *perichoresis*: He communicates within himself, and he communicates himself to us. This is the beginning of communication. To communicate is precisely to draw from the Being of God and to have the same attitude. It is not being able to remain alone. It is the need to communicate what I have and think is the true, the just, the good, and the beautiful. We communicate with the soul and with the body. We communicate with the mind, with the heart, with the hands. We communicate with everything. The true communicator gives everything, gives all of himself or herself, does not hold something back for himself or herself. And it is true that the greatest communication is love. In love there is the fullness of communication: love of God and of one another.

IN THE EUCHARIST, GOD COMMUNICATES HIMSELF AS LOVE

In the Eucharist[3], the Lord's love for us is communicated: a love so great that it feeds us with himself, a gratuitous love, always at the disposal of every person who is hungry and in need of regenerating his or her strength. Living the experience of faith means letting oneself be nourished by the Lord and building one's existence not on material goods, but on the reality that does not perish — the gifts of God, his Word and his Body.

FROM THE LOVE OF GOD TO THE LOVE OF OUR BROTHERS AND SISTERS

By[4] receiving him in Communion, we receive his life within us, and we become children of the heavenly Father and brothers among ourselves. By receiving Communion, we meet Jesus truly living and risen! Taking part in the Eucharist means entering into the logic of Jesus, the logic of giving freely, of sharing. And as poor as we are, we all have something to give. To receive Communion means to draw from Christ the grace which enables us to share with others all we are and all we have.

THE PRIMACY OF RELATIONSHIPS

From[5] the contemplation of the very mystery of the Trinity of God and the Incarnation of the Son springs the primacy given by Christian thought and the Church's action to relationships, to the encounter with the sacred mystery of the other, to universal communion with all of humanity as the vocation of all.

JESUS IS THE GOOD NEWS OF THE FATHER

Jesus[6] is himself the fulfillment of those promises; he himself is the "good news" to believe in, to receive, and to communicate to all men and women of every time that they too may entrust their life to him. Jesus Christ, in his person, is the Word living and working in history: Whoever hears and follows him may enter the kingdom of God.

JESUS LOOKS ON US WITH LOVE

Let us[7] recall the three verbs in this evocative photogram: to see, to have compassion, to teach. We can call them the verbs of the Shepherd: to see, to have compassion, to teach. The first and second, to see and to have compassion, are always found together in the attitude of Jesus; in fact, his gaze is not the gaze of a sociologist or a photojournalist, for he always gazes with "the eyes of the heart." These two verbs, to see and to have compassion, configure Jesus as the Good Shepherd. His compassion, too, is not merely a human feeling, but is the deep emotion of the Messiah in whom God's tenderness is made flesh. From this tenderness is born Jesus' wish to nourish the crowd with the bread of his Word — that is, to teach the Word of God to the people. Jesus sees, Jesus has compassion, Jesus teaches us.

JESUS CRUCIFIED COMMUNICATES TO US THE VICTORY OF LOVE

Jesus' eyes[8] [in the image of the Crucifix of San Damiano] are not closed but open, wide open: He looks at us in a way that touches our hearts. The cross does not speak to us about defeat and failure; paradoxically, it speaks to us about a death which is life, a death which gives life, for it speaks to us of love, the love of God incarnate, a love which does not die, but triumphs over evil and death. When we let the crucified Jesus gaze upon us, we are re-created, we become "a new creation."

SHARED BEAUTY

Just[9] as God has made the work of his creation available to human beings, so human beings themselves find their full realization by giving life to a "shared beauty." We are faced with a "key" of the universe, on which its survival also depends: This key is the plan of God's covenant. It is a question of recognizing the intention that is written in the beauty of creation, which is the Creator's desire to communicate, to offer a wonderful message to those who can interpret it — that is, we human beings.

THE TRUTH IS A RELATIONSHIP

The truth,[10] according to the Christian faith, is God's love for us in Jesus Christ. Therefore, the truth is a relationship! So much so that all of us grasp the truth and express it starting from ourselves: our history and culture, the situation in which we live, etc. This does not mean that truth is variable and subjective — quite the contrary. But it does mean that it is always and uniquely given to us as a path and a life. Didn't Jesus himself say, "I am the way, the truth, and the life"? In other words, since truth is ultimately one with love, it requires humility and openness to be sought out, welcomed, and expressed.

WHAT IS THE TRUTH?

Does[11] "the" truth really exist? What is "the" truth? Can we know it? Can we find it? Here springs to my mind the question of Pontius Pilate, the Roman procurator, when Jesus reveals to him the deep meaning of his mission: "What is truth?" (Jn 18:37, 38). Pilate cannot understand that "the" Truth is standing in front of him, he cannot see in Jesus the face of the truth that is the face of God. And yet Jesus is exactly this: the Truth that, in the fullness of time, "became flesh" (see Jn 1:1, 14) and came to dwell among us so that we might know it. The truth is not grasped as a thing, the truth is encountered. It is not a possession, it is an encounter with a Person. ... Then, as Jesus promised, the Holy Spirit guides us "into all the truth" (Jn 16:13); not only does he guide us to the encounter with Jesus, the fullness of the Truth, but he also guides us "into" the Truth — that is, he makes us enter into an ever-deeper communion with Jesus, giving us knowledge of all the things of God. And we cannot achieve this by our own efforts. Unless God enlightens us from within, our Christian existence will be superficial. ... May Christ's truth, which the Holy Spirit teaches us and gives to us, always and totally affect our daily lives. Let us call on him more often so that he may guide us on the path of disciples of Christ. Let us call on him every day. I am making this suggestion to you: Let us invoke the Holy Spirit every day; in this way the Holy Spirit will bring us close to Jesus Christ.

JESUS IS THE TRUTH

Truth[12] is fully realized in the very person of Jesus (see Jn 14:6), in his way of living and of dying, in the fruit of his relationship with the Father. This existence as children of God, he, the Risen One, gives it to us too, sending the Holy Spirit who is the Spirit of truth, who attests to our heart that God is our Father (Rom 8:16).

In every action, man, people, either affirm or deny this truth, from the little everyday situations to the most binding choices. But the logic is always the same, what our parents and grandparents teach us when they tell us not to tell lies. ... The truth is the marvelous revelation of God, of his fatherly face; it is his boundless love. This truth corresponds to human reason, but infinitely transcends it, because it is a gift descended to the earth and embodied in Christ crucified and risen; it is made visible by those who belong to him and demonstrate his same disposition.

Not bearing false witness means living as children of God, who never, ever contradict themselves, never tell lies; living as children of God; letting shine forth in every deed the supreme truth: that God is Father and that we can trust in him. I trust God: This is the great truth. From our trust in God — who is Father and who loves me, loves us — springs my truth, being truthful and not a liar.

THE SPIRIT URGES US ON

Like[13] on the day of Pentecost, the Holy Spirit is continually being poured out on the Church and on each one of us so that we may come out of our mediocrity and our closures and communicate the Lord's merciful love to the whole world. To communicate the Lord's merciful love: This is our mission! We, too, are given the gift of the "tongue" of the Gospel and the "fire" of the Holy Spirit, so that as we proclaim the risen Jesus, alive and present among us, we may warm our hearts and the hearts of peoples, bringing them closer to him, the way, the truth, and the life.

FAITH IS LETTING OURSELVES BE DRAWN BY THE FATHER

Faith,[14] which is like a seed deep in the heart, blossoms when we let the Father draw us to Jesus, and we "go to him" with an open heart, without prejudices; then we recognize in his face the Face of God, and in his words the Word of God, because the Holy Spirit has made us enter into the relationship of love and of life between Jesus and God the Father. And there we receive a gift, the gift of the Faith.

PROCLAIMING THE FAITH MEANS ENGAGING IN RELATIONSHIPS

Faith,[15] in fact, needs a setting in which it can be witnessed to and communicated, a means which is suitable and proportionate to what is communicated. For transmitting a purely doctrinal content, an idea might suffice, or perhaps a book, or the repetition of a spoken message. But what is communicated in the Church, what is handed down in her living Tradition, is the new light born of an encounter with the true God, a light which touches us at the core of our being and engages our minds, wills, and emotions, opening us to relationships lived in communion. There is a special means for passing down this fullness, a means capable of engaging the entire person, body and spirit, interior life and relationships, with others. It is the sacraments, celebrated in the Church's liturgy. The sacraments communicate an incarnate memory, linked to the times and places of our lives, linked to all our senses; in them the whole person is engaged as a member of a living subject and part of a network of communitarian relationships.

FAITH ILLUMINATES ALL HUMAN RELATIONSHIPS

Christian[16] faith, inasmuch as it proclaims the truth of God's total love and opens us to the power of that love, penetrates to the core of our human experience. Each of us comes to the light because of love, and each of us is called to love in order to remain in the light. Desirous of illuminating all reality with the love of God made manifest in Jesus, and seeking to love others with that same love, the first Christians found in the Greek world, with its thirst for truth, an ideal partner in dialogue. The encounter of the Gospel message with the philosophical culture of the ancient world proved a decisive step in the evangelization of all peoples, and stimulated a fruitful interaction between faith and reason which has continued down the centuries to our own times. St. John Paul II, in his encyclical letter *Fides et Ratio*, showed how faith and reason each strengthen the other. Once we discover the full light of Christ's love, we realize that each of the loves in our own lives had always contained a ray of that light, and we understand its ultimate destination. The fact that our human loves contain that ray of light also helps us to see how all love is meant to share in the complete self-gift of the Son of God for our sake. In this circular movement, the light of faith illumines all our human relationships, which can then be lived in union with the gentle love of Christ.

DAILY ... TOGETHER*

NAZARETH

Each[1] Christian family can — as Mary and Joseph did — welcome Jesus, listen to him, speak with him, guard him, protect him, grow with him; and in this way improve the world. Let us make room in our heart and in our day for the Lord. As Mary and Joseph also did, and it was not easy: how many difficulties they had to overcome! They were not a superficial family; they were not an unreal family. The family of Nazareth urges us to rediscover the vocation and mission of the family, of every family. And what happened in those thirty years in Nazareth can thus happen to us, too: seeking to make love and not hate normal, making mutual help commonplace,

*We reproduce here selections from the catechesis on family relationships given by Pope Francis during the Wednesday general audiences from December 10, 2014, to September 16, 2015.

not indifference or enmity. It is no coincidence, then, that "Nazareth" means "She who keeps," as Mary, who — as the Gospel states — "kept all these things in her heart" (see Lk 2:19, 51). Since then, each time there is a family that keeps this mystery, even if it were on the periphery of the world, the mystery of the Son of God, the mystery of Jesus who comes to save us, the mystery is at work. He comes to save the world. And this is the great mission of the family: to make room for Jesus who is coming, to welcome Jesus in the family, in each member — children, husband, wife, grandparents. … Jesus is there. Welcome him there, in order that he grow spiritually in the family. May the Lord grant us this grace in these last days of Advent.

MOTHERS
Let[2] us continue with the catechesis on the family, and in the family there is the mother. Every human person owes his or her life to a mother, and almost always owes much of what follows in life, both human and spiritual formation, to her. Yet, despite being highly lauded from a symbolic point of view — many poems, many beautiful things said poetically of her — the mother is rarely listened to or helped in daily life, rarely considered central to society in her role. Rather, often the readiness of mothers to make sacrifices for their children is taken advantage of so as to "save" on social spending.

It also happens that in Christian communities the mother is not always held in the right regard; she is barely heard. Yet the center of the life of the Church is the mother of Jesus. Perhaps mothers, ready to sacrifice so much for their children, and often for others as well, ought to be listened to more. We should understand more about their daily struggle to be efficient at work and attentive and affectionate in the family; we should better grasp what they aspire to in order to express the best and most authentic fruits of their emancipation. A mother with her children always has problems, always work. I remember there were five of us children at home, and while one was doing one thing, the other wanted to do another, and our poor mama went back and forth from one's side to another, but she was happy. She gave us so much.

Mothers are the strongest antidote to the spread of self-centered individualism. "Individual" means "what cannot be divided." Mothers, instead, "divide" themselves, from the moment they bear a child, to give him to the world and help him grow. It is they, mothers, who most hate war, which kills their children. Many times, I have thought of those mothers who receive the letter: "I inform you that your son has fallen in defense of his homeland. …" The poor women! How a mother suffers! It is they who testify to the beauty of life. Archbishop Oscar Arnulfo Romero said that mothers experience a "maternal martyrdom." In the homily for the funeral of a priest assassinated by death squads, he said, recalling the Second Vatican Council:

> We must be ready to die for our faith, even if the Lord does not grant us this honor. … Giving one's life does not only mean being killed; giving one's life, having the spirit of a martyr, it is in giving in duty, in silence, in prayer, in honest fulfillment of his duty, in that silence of daily life; giving one's life little by little. Yes, like it is given by a mother, who without fear and with

the simplicity of the maternal martyrdom conceives
a child in her womb, gives birth to him, nurses him,
helps them grow and cares for them with affection.
She gives her life. That's martyrdom.

Yes, being a mother doesn't only mean bringing a child to the world, but it is also a life choice. What does a mother choose, what is the life choice of a mother? The life choice of a mother is the choice to give life. And this is great, this is beautiful.

A society without mothers would be a dehumanized society, for mothers are always, even in the worst moments, witnesses of tenderness, dedication, and moral strength. Mothers often pass on the deepest sense of religious practice: In a human being's life, the value of faith is inscribed in the first prayers, the first acts of devotion that a child learns. It is a message that believing mothers are able to pass on without much explanation — these come later, but the seed of faith is those early precious moments. Without mothers, not only would there be no new faithful, but the Faith would lose a good part of its simple and profound warmth. And the Church is mother, with all of this; she is our mother! We are not orphans, we have a mother! Our Lady, mother Church, is our mom. We are not orphans, we are children of the Church, we are children of Our Lady, and we are children of our mothers.

Dearest mothers, thank you, thank you for what you are in your family and for what you give to the Church and the world. And to you, beloved Church, thank you, thank you for being mother. And to you, Mary, Mother of God, thank you for letting us see Jesus.

FATHERS (I)

"Father"[3] is a term familiar to everyone, a universal word. It indicates a fundamental relationship, the reality of which is as old as human history. Today, however, one has reached the point of claiming that our society is a "society without fathers." In other words, particularly in Western culture, the father figure would be symbolically absent, paled, removed. At first, this was perceived as a liberation: liberation from the father-master, from the father as the representative of the law that is imposed from without, from the father as the censor of his children's happiness and the obstacle to the emancipation and autonomy of young people. At times in some homes authoritarianism reigned in the past, in some cases even oppression: parents who treated their children like servants, not respecting their individual needs for growth; fathers who did not help them to start out on their journey with freedom — and it is not easy to bring up a child in freedom; fathers who did not help them assume their own responsibilities to build their future and that of society.

This, certainly, is not a good approach; but, as often happens, one goes from one extreme to the other. In our day, the problem no longer seems to be the invasive presence of the father so much as his absence, his inaction. Fathers are sometimes so concentrated on themselves, and on their work, and at times on their career that they even forget about the family. And they leave the little ones and the young ones to themselves. As bishop of Buenos Aires, in Argentina, I sensed the feeling of orphanhood that children are experiencing today, and I often asked fathers if they played with their children, if they had the courage and love to spend time with their kids. And the answer was negative in most cases: "But I can't, because I have so much work ..." And the father was absent from the little child growing up, he did not play with him, no, he did not waste time with him.

Now, on this common journey of reflection on the family, I would like to say to all Christian communities that we must be more attentive: The absent father figure in the life of little ones and young people causes gaps and wounds that may even be very serious. And, in effect, delinquency among children and adolescents can be largely attributed to this lack, to the shortage of examples and authoritative guidance in their everyday life, a shortage of closeness, a shortage of love from the father. And the feeling of orphanhood that so many young people live with is more profound than we think.

They are orphaned in the family, because their fathers are often absent, also physically, from the home, but above all because, when they are present, they do not behave like fathers. They do not converse with their children. They do not fulfill their role as educators. They do not set their children a good example with their words, principles, values, those rules of life which they need like bread. The educative quality of the time the father spends raising the child is all the more necessary when he is forced to stay away from home because of work. Sometimes it seems that fathers don't know what their role in the family is or how to raise their children. So, in doubt, they abstain, they retreat and neglect their responsibilities, perhaps taking refuge in the unlikely relationship as "equals" with their children. It's true that you have to be a "companion" to your child, but without forgetting that you are the father! If you behave only as a peer to your child, it will do him or her no good.

And we also see this problem in the civil community. The civil community with its institutions, has a certain — let's call it paternal — responsibility toward young people, a responsibility that at times is neglected or poorly exercised. It too often leaves them orphaned and does not offer them a true perspective. Young people are thus deprived of safe paths to follow, of teachers to trust in, of ideals to warm their hearts, of values, and of hopes to sustain them daily. They become filled perhaps with idols, but their hearts are robbed; they are obliged to dream of amusement and pleasure, but they are not given work; they become deluded by the god of money, and they are denied true wealth.

And so it would do everyone good, fathers and children, to listen again to the promise that Jesus made to his disciples: "I will not leave you orphans" (Jn 14:18). He is, indeed, the Way to follow, the Teacher to listen to, the Hope that the world can change, that love conquers hatred, that there can be a future of brotherhood and peace for all.

FATHERS (II)

Every[4] family needs a father. Today we shall reflect on the value of his role, and I would like to begin with a few expressions that we find in the Book of Proverbs, words that a father addresses to his own son, and it reads like this: "My son, if your heart is wise, / my heart too will be glad. / My soul will rejoice / when your lips speak what is right" (23:15–16). Nothing could better express the pride and emotion a father feels when he understands that he has handed down to his child what really matters in life — that is, a wise heart. This father does not say: "I am proud of you because you are the same as me, because you repeat the things I say and do." No, he does not say anything so simple to him. He says something much more important, which we can understand in this way: "I will be happy every time I see you act with wisdom, and I will be moved every time that I hear you speak with rectitude. This is what I wanted to leave to you, that this one thing become yours: the attitude to feel and act, to speak and judge with wisdom and rectitude. And that you might be like this, [that] I taught you the things you didn't know, I corrected the errors you didn't see. I made you feel a profound and at the same time discrete affection, which maybe you did not fully recognize when you were young and unsure. I gave you a testimony of rigor and steadfastness that perhaps you didn't understand when you would have liked only complicity and protection. I had first to test myself in the wisdom of my heart, be vigilant of my excesses of sentiment and resentment, in order to carry the weight of the inevitable misunderstandings, to find the right words to make myself understood." Now, continues the father, "I see that you strive to be this way with your own children, and with everyone, and it moves me. I am happy to be your father." This is what a wise father, a mature father, says. A father knows all too well what it costs to hand down this heritage: how close, how gentle, and how firm to be. But what consolation and what recompense he receives when the children honor this legacy! It is a joy that rewards all the toil, that overcomes every misunderstanding and heals every wound.

The first need, then, is precisely this: that a father be present in the family. That he be close to his wife, to share everything, joy and sorrow, hope and hardship. And that he be close to his children as they grow — when they play and when they strive, when they are carefree and when they are distressed, when they are talkative and when they are silent, when they are daring and when they are afraid, when they take a wrong step and when they find their path again — a father who is always present. To say "present" is not to say "controlling"! Fathers who are too controlling cancel out their children, they don't let them develop.

The Gospel speaks to us about the exemplarity of the Father who is in heaven — who alone, Jesus says, can be truly called the "good Father" (see Mk 10:18). Everyone knows that extraordinary parable of the "prodigal son," or better yet of the "merciful father," which we find in the Gospel of Luke (15:11–32). What dignity and what tenderness there is in the expectation of that father, who stands at the door of the house waiting for his son to return! Fathers must be patient. Often there is nothing else to do but wait; pray and wait with patience, gentleness, magnanimity, and mercy.

A good father knows how to wait and knows how to forgive from the depths of his heart. Certainly, he also knows how to correct with firmness: He is not a weak father, submissive and sentimental. The father who knows how to correct without humiliating is the one who knows how to protect without sparing himself. Once I heard a father at a meeting on marriage say, "Sometimes I have to strike the children lightly ... but never in the face so as not to humiliate them." How beautiful! He has a sense of dignity. He must punish, but he does it in a just way, and moves on.

If then there is someone who can fully explain the prayer of the Our Father, taught by Jesus, it is the one who lives out paternity in the first person. Without the grace that comes from the Father who is in heaven, fathers lose courage and abandon camp. But children need to find a father waiting for them when they come home after failing. They will do everything not to admit it, not to show it, but they need it, and not to find it opens wounds in them that are difficult to heal.

The Church, our mother, is committed to supporting with all her strength the good and generous presence of fathers in families, for they are the irreplaceable guardians and mediators of faith in goodness, of faith in justice, and in God's protection, like Saint Joseph.

SONS AND DAUGHTERS

In[5] this catechesis on the family I would like to talk about the child, or even better, about children. I shall use a beautiful image from Isaiah. The prophet writes: "They all gather together, they come to you; / your sons shall come from far, / and your daughters shall be carried in the arms. / Then you shall see and be radiant, / your heart shall thrill and rejoice" (Is 60:4–5). It is a splendid image, an image of happiness which is fulfilled in the reunion of parents and children, who journey together toward a future of freedom and peace, after a long period of deprivation and separation, when the Hebrew people were far from their homeland.

In essence, there is a close link between the hope of a people and the harmony among generations. We must consider this carefully. There is a close link between the hope of a people and the harmony among generations. The joy of children causes the parents' hearts to beat and reopens the future. Children are the joy of the family and of society. They are not a question of reproductive biology, nor one of the many ways to fulfill oneself, much less a possession of their parents. ... No. Children are a gift, they are a gift: Understood? Children are a gift. Each one is unique and irreplaceable, and at the same time unmistakably linked to his/her roots. In fact, according to God's plan, being son and daughter means to carry within oneself the memory and hope of a love which was fulfilled in the very kindling of the life of another, original and new, human being. And for parents each child is original, different, diverse. Allow me to share a family memory. I remember what my mother said about us (there were five of us): "I have five children." When they asked her: "Which one is your favorite," she answered: "I have five children, like five fingers. [He displays his fingers] Should they strike this one, it hurts me; should they strike that one, it hurts me. All five hurt me. All are my children, and all are different like the fingers of a hand." And this is how a family is! The children are all different, but all children.

A child is loved because he is one's child: not because he is beautiful, or because he is like this or like that; no, because he is a child! Not because he thinks as I do or embodies my dreams. A child is a child: a life generated by us but intended for him, for his good, for the good of the family, of society, of mankind as a whole.

From this also derives the depth of the human experience of being son or daughter, which allows us to discover the most gratuitous dimension of love, which never ceases to astonish us. It is the beauty of being loved first: Children are loved before they arrive. So often I find mothers in the square who are expecting a baby and ask me for a blessing

... these babies are loved before coming into the world. And this is free, this is love; they are loved before being born, like the love of God who always loves us first. They are loved before having done anything to deserve it, before knowing how to talk or think, even before coming into the world! Being children is the basic condition for knowing the love of God, which is the ultimate source of this authentic miracle. In the soul of every child, inasmuch as it is vulnerable, God places the seal of this love, which is at the basis of his/her personal dignity, a dignity which nothing and no one can ever destroy.

Today it seems more difficult for children to imagine their future. Fathers — I touched on this in previous catechesis — have perhaps taken a step backward, and children have become more uncertain in taking their steps forward. We can learn the good relationship between generations from our heavenly Father, who leaves each of us free but never leaves us on our own. And if we err, he continues to follow us with patience, without abating his love for us. Our heavenly Father does not take steps back in his love for us, ever! He always goes forward, and if he cannot go forward he waits for us, but he never goes backward; he wants his children to be brave and take their steps forward.

The children, for their part, must not be afraid of the task of building a new world: It is right for them to want to improve on what they have received! But this must be done without arrogance, without presumption. One must know how to recognize a child's virtue, and parents always deserve honor.

The Fourth Commandment asks children — we are all children! — to honor our father and mother (see Ex 20:12). This commandment comes immediately after those regarding God himself. Indeed, it contains something sacred, something divine, something which lies at the root of every other type of respect among men. And to the biblical formulation of the Fourth Commandment is added: "that your days may be long in the land which the Lord your God gives you." The virtuous bond between generations is the guarantee of the future and is the guarantee of a truly human history. A society with children who do not honor parents is a society without honor; when one does not honor one's parents, one loses one's own honor! It is a society destined to be filled with arid and avid young people. However, even a society with a paucity of generations, which does not love being surrounded by children, which considers them above all a worry, a weight, a risk, is a depressed society. Let us consider the many societies we know here in Europe: They are depressed societies, because they do not want children, they are not having children — the birth rate does not reach 1 percent. Why? Let each of us consider and respond.

If a family with many children is looked upon as a weight, something is wrong! The child's generation must be responsible, as the encyclical *Humanae Vitae*, by Pope St. Paul VI, also teaches, but having many children cannot automatically be an irresponsible choice. Not to have children is a selfish choice. Life is rejuvenated and acquires energy by multiplying: It is enriched, not impoverished! Children learn to assume responsibility for their family. They mature in sharing its hardship. They grow in the appreciation of its gifts. The happy experience of brotherhood inspires respect and care for parents, to whom our recognition is due. So many of you present here have children, and we are all children. Let us do something, let us observe a moment of silence. Each of us think in our heart about our children — if we have any — think in silence. And let us all think about our parents and thank God for the gift of life. In silence, those who have children think of them, and everyone think of our parents. (Silence). May the Lord bless our parents and bless your children.

BROTHERS AND SISTERS

"Brother"[6] and "sister" are words that Christianity really loves. And, thanks to the family experience, they are words that all cultures and all times comprehend.

The fraternal bond holds a special place in the history of the People of God, who received his revelation at the core of the human experience. The psalmist sings of the beauty of the fraternal bond: "Behold, how good and pleasant it is / when brothers dwell in unity!" (Ps 133:1). And this is true, brotherhood is beautiful! Jesus Christ also brought to its fullness this human experience of being brothers and sisters, embracing it in Trinitarian love and thereby empowering it to go well beyond the ties of kinship and enabling it to surmount every barrier of extraneousness.

We know that when the fraternal relationship is destroyed, when the relationship between siblings is destroyed, the road is open to painful experiences of conflict, of betrayal, of hate. The biblical account of Cain and Abel is an example of this negative outcome. After the killing of Abel, God asks Cain: "Where is Abel your brother?" (Gn 4:9). It is a question that the Lord continues to repeat to every generation. And, unfortunately, in every generation Cain's dramatic answer never fails to be repeated: "I do not know; am I my brother's keeper?" (4:9). The rupture of the bond between siblings is a nasty, bad thing for humanity. In the family, too, how many siblings quarrel over little things, or over an inheritance, and then they no longer speak to each other, they no longer greet one another. This is terrible! Brotherhood is a great thing, when we consider that all our brothers and sisters lived in the womb of the same mother for nine months, came from the mother's flesh! Brotherhood cannot be broken. Let us consider: We all know families that have divided siblings, who have quarreled; let us ask the Lord — perhaps in our family there are a few cases — to help these families to reunite their siblings, to rebuild the family. Brotherhood must not be broken, and when it breaks, what happened to Cain and Abel occurs. When the Lord asks Cain where his brother is, he replies: "I do not know, my brother does not matter to me." This is terrible, it is a very, very painful thing to hear. In our prayers let us always pray for siblings who are at odds.

Should the bond of fraternity which forms in the family between children arise in an educational atmosphere of openness to others, it is the great school of freedom and peace. In the family, among siblings, human coexistence is learned, how one must live in society. Perhaps we are not always aware of it, but the family itself introduces fraternity into the world! Beginning with this first experience of fraternity, nourished by affection and education at home, the style of fraternity radiates like a promise upon the whole of society and on its relations among peoples.

The blessing that God, in Jesus Christ, pours out on this bond of fraternity expands in an unimaginable way. He renders it capable of overcoming all differences of nationality, language, culture, and even religion.

Consider what becomes of the bond between men and women, even when completely different from each other, when they are able to say of another: "He is truly like a brother, she is just like a sister to me." This is beautiful! History has shown well enough, after all, that even freedom and equality, without brotherhood, can be full of individualism and conformism, and even personal interests.

Familial fraternity shines in a special way when we see the care, the patience, the affection that envelop the weakest little brother or sister, sick or physically challenged. There are countless brothers and sisters who do this, throughout the world, and perhaps we do not appreciate their generosity enough. And when there are many siblings in a family — today, I greeted a family that has nine children — the eldest boy or girl helps the dad, the mom, to take care of the younger children. This work of helping among siblings is beautiful.

Having a brother, a sister, who loves you is a deep, precious, irreplaceable experience. Christian fraternity happens in the same way. The smallest, the weakest, the poorest soften us: They have the "right" to take our heart and soul. Yes, they are our brothers and sisters, and as such we must love and care for them. When this happens, when the poor are like family members, our own Christian fraternity comes to life again. Christians, in fact, go to meet the poor and the weak not to obey an ideological program, but because the word and the example of the Lord tell us that we are all brothers and sisters. This is the principle of God's love and of all justice among men. I should like to suggest something before concluding, just a few words, in silence, each of us, let us think of our brothers, our sisters, and from our heart let us pray in silence for them. A moment of silence.

Here then, with this prayer we have brought all, brothers and sisters, with our thoughts, with our hearts, here to [St. Peter's] Square to receive the blessing.

Today more than ever it is necessary to place fraternity back at the center of our technocratic and bureaucratic society: Then even freedom and equality will find the correct balance. Therefore, let us not thoughtlessly deprive our families, out of criticism or fear, of the beauty of a bountiful fraternal experience of sons and daughters. And let us not lose our trust in the broad horizon faith is able to draw from this experience, enlightened by God's blessing.

GRANDPARENTS

When[7] I was in the Philippines, the Filipino people greeted me saying "Lolo Kiko" — meaning Grandpa Francis — "Lolo Kiko," they said! The first important thing to stress: It is true that society tends to discard us, but the Lord definitely does not! The Lord never discards us. He calls us to follow him in every age of life, and old age has a grace and a mission too, a true vocation from the Lord. Old age is a vocation. It is not yet time to "pull in the oars." This period of life is different from those before, there is no doubt; we even have to somewhat "invent it ourselves," because our societies are not ready, spiritually and morally, to appreciate the true value of this stage of life. Indeed, it once was not so normal to have time available; it is much more so today. Christian spirituality has also been caught somewhat by surprise with regard to outlining a kind of spirituality of the elderly. But thanks be to

God there is no shortage of the testimony of elderly saints, both men and women!

I was really moved by the "Day Dedicated to the Elderly" that we had here in St. Peter's Square last year, [which] was full. I listened to the stories of elderly people who devote themselves to others, and to stories of married couples, who said, "We are celebrating our fiftieth wedding anniversary; we are celebrating our sixtieth wedding anniversary." It is important to present this to young people who tire so easily; the testimony of the elderly in fidelity is important. There were so many in this Square that day. It is a reflection to continue, in both the ecclesial and civil spheres. The Gospel comes to meet us with a really moving and encouraging image. It is the image of Simeon and Anna, who are spoken of in the Gospel of Jesus' childhood, composed by Saint Luke. There were certainly elderly: (the "old man") Simeon, and the "prophetess," Anna, who was eighty-four years old. This woman did not hide her age. The Gospel says that they awaited the coming of God every day, with great trust, for many years. They truly wanted to see him that day, to grasp the signs, to understand the origin. By then, they were also perhaps more resigned to die first: That long wait, however, continued to occupy their whole life, having no commitments more important than ... to await the Lord and pray. So, when Mary and Joseph went to the Temple to fulfill the provisions of the Law, Simeon and Anna moved quickly, inspired by the Holy Spirit (see Lk 2:27). The burden of age and waiting disappeared in an instant. They recognized the Child, and discovered new strength, for a new task: to give thanks for and bear witness to this sign from God. Simeon improvised a beautiful hymn of jubilation

(2:29–32) — in that moment he was a poet — and Anna became the first woman to preach of Jesus: She "spoke of him to all who were looking for the redemption of Jerusalem" (2:38).

Dear grandparents, dear elderly, let us follow in the footsteps of these extraordinary elders! Let us, too, become like poets of prayer: Let us develop a taste for finding our own words, let us once again grasp those which teach us the Word of God. The prayer of grandparents and of the elderly is a great gift for the Church. The prayer of grandparents and of the elderly is a great gift for the Church, it is a treasure! A great injection of wisdom for the whole of human society: above all for one which is too busy, too taken, too distracted. Someone should also sing, for them too, sing of the signs of God, proclaim the signs of God, pray for them! Let us look to Benedict XVI, who chose to spend the final span of his life in prayer and listening to God. This is beautiful! A great believer of the last century of the Orthodox tradition, Olivier Clément, said: "A civilization which has no place for prayer is a civilization in which old age has lost all meaning. And this is terrifying. For, above all, we need old people who pray; prayer is the purpose of old age." We need old people who pray because this is the very purpose of old age. The prayer of the elderly is a beautiful thing.

We are able to thank the Lord for the benefits received and fill the emptiness of ingratitude that surrounds us. We are able to intercede for the expectations of younger generations and give dignity to the memory and sacrifices of past generations. We are able to remind ambitious young people that a life without love is a barren life. We are able to say to young people who are afraid that anxiety about the future can be overcome. We are able to teach the young who are overly self-absorbed that there is more joy in giving than in receiving. Grandfathers and grandmothers form the enduring "chorus" of a great spiritual sanctuary, where prayers of supplication and songs of praise sustain the community which toils and struggles in the field of life.

Last, prayer unceasingly purifies the heart. Praise and supplication to God prevents the heart from becoming hardened by resentment and selfishness. How awful is the cynicism of an elderly person who has lost the meaning of his testimony, who scorns the young and does not communicate the wisdom of life! How beautiful, however, is the encouragement an elderly person manages to pass on to a young person who is seeking the meaning of faith and of life! It is truly the mission of grandparents, the vocation of the elderly. The words of grandparents have special value for the young. And the young know it. I still carry with me, always, in my breviary, the words my grandmother consigned to me in writing on the day of my priestly ordination. I read them often and they do me good.

How I would like a Church that challenges the throw-away culture with the overflowing joy of a new embrace between young and old! This is what I ask of the Lord today, this embrace.

CHILDREN

I[8] would like to conclude this first group of catecheses on the family by speaking about children. ... Today I will focus on the great gift that children are for humanity — it is true they are a great gift for humanity, but also really excluded because they are not even allowed to be born. ... Who come to mind are the many children I met during my recent journey to Asia: full of life, of enthusiasm, and, on the other hand, I see that in the world, many of them live in unworthy conditions. ... In fact, from the way children are treated society can be judged, not only morally but also sociologically, whether it is a liberal society or a society enslaved by international interests.

First of all, children remind us that we all, in the first years of life, were completely dependent upon the care and benevolence of others. The Son of God was not spared this stage. It is the mystery that we contemplate every year at Christmas. The Nativity scene is the icon which communicates this reality in the simplest and most direct way. It is curious: God has no difficulty in making himself understood by children, and children have no difficulty in understanding God. It is not by chance that in the Gospel there are several very beautiful and powerful words of Jesus regarding the "little ones." This term, "babes," refers to all the people who depend on the help of others, and to children in particular. For example, Jesus says, "I thank thee, Father, Lord of heaven and earth, that thou hast hidden these things from the wise and understanding, and revealed them to babes" (Mt 11:25). And again, "See that you do not despise one of these little ones: for I tell you that in heaven their angels always behold the face of my Father who is in heaven" (Mt 18:10).

Thus children are in and of themselves a treasure for humanity and also for the Church, for they constantly evoke that necessary condition for entering the kingdom of God: that of not considering ourselves self-sufficient, but in need of help, of love, of forgiveness. We all are in need of help, of love, and of forgiveness! Children remind us of another beautiful thing: They remind us that we are always sons and daughters. Even if one becomes an adult, or an elderly person, even if one becomes a parent, if one occupies a position of responsibility, underneath all of this is still the identity of a child. We are all sons and daughters. And this always brings us back to the fact that we did not give ourselves life, but that we received it. The great gift of life is the first gift that we received. Sometimes in life we risk forgetting about this, as if we were the masters of our existence, and instead we are fundamentally dependent. In reality, it is a motive of great joy to feel at every stage of life, in every situation, in every social condition, that we are, and we remain, sons and daughters. This is the main message that children give us by their very presence: Simply by their presence they remind us that each and every one of us is a son or daughter.

But there are so many gifts, so many riches that children bring to humanity. I shall mention only a few.

They bring their way of seeing reality, with a trusting and pure gaze. A child has spontaneous trust in his father and mother; he has spontaneous trust in God, in Jesus, in Our Lady. At the same time, his interior gaze is pure, not yet tainted by malice, by duplicity, by the "incrustations" of life which harden the heart. We know that children are also marked by original sin, that they are selfish, but they preserve purity, and interior simplicity. But children are not diplomats: They say what they feel, say what they see, directly. And so often they put their parents in difficulty, saying in front of other people, "I don't like this because it is ugly." But children say what they see, they are not two-faced, they have not yet learned that science of duplicity that we adults have unfortunately learned.

Furthermore, children — in their interior simplicity — bring with them the capacity to receive and give tenderness. Tenderness is having a heart "of flesh" and not "of stone," as the Bible says (see Ez 36:26). Tenderness is also poetry: It is "feeling" things and events, not treating them as mere objects, only to use them, because they are useful. ...

Children have the capacity to smile and to cry. Some, when I pick them up to embrace them, smile; others see me dressed in white and think I am a doctor and that I am going to vaccinate them, and they cry ... spontaneously! Children are like this, they smile and cry, two things which are often "stifled" in grown-ups; we are no longer capable. ... So often our smile becomes a cardboard smile, fixed, a smile that is not natural, even an artificial smile, like a clown. Children smile spontaneously and cry spontaneously. It always depends on the heart, and often our heart is blocked and loses this capacity to smile, to cry. So, children can teach us how to smile and cry again. But we must ask ourselves: Do I smile spontaneously, frankly, with love, or is my smile artificial? Do I still cry, or have I lost the capacity to cry? These are two very human questions that children teach us.

For all these reasons Jesus invited his disciples to "become like children," because "the kingdom of God belongs to those who are like them" (see Mt 18:3; Mk 10:14).

Dear brothers and sisters, children bring life, cheerfulness, hope, also troubles. But such is life. Certainly, they also bring worries and sometimes many problems; but better a society with these worries and these problems than a sad, gray society because it is without children! When we see that the birth rate of a society is barely 1 percent, we can say that this society is sad, it is gray because it has no children.

MEN AND WOMEN (I)

Today's[9] catechesis is dedicated to an aspect central to the theme of the family: the great gift that God gave to humanity with the creation of man and woman and with the sacrament of marriage. This catechesis and the next one will treat the difference and complementarity between man and woman, who stand at the summit of divine creation. ...

Let us begin with a brief comment on the first narrative of creation, in the Book of Genesis. Here we read that God, after having created the universe and all living beings, created his masterpiece, the human being, whom he made in his own image: "In the image of God he created them; / male and female he created them" (Gn 1:27).

And as we all know, sexual difference is present in so many forms of life, on the great scale of living beings. But man and woman alone are made in the image and likeness of God: The biblical text repeats it three times in two passages (see Gn 1:26–27): Man and woman are the image and likeness of God. This tells us that it is not man alone who is the image of God or woman alone who is the image of God, but man and woman as a couple who are the image of God. The difference between man and woman is not meant to stand in opposition, or to subordinate, but is for the sake of communion and generation, always in the image and likeness of God.

Experience teaches us: In order to know oneself well and

develop harmoniously, a human being needs the reciprocity of man and woman. When that is lacking, one can see the consequences. We are made to listen to one another and help one another. We can say that without the mutual enrichment of this relationship — in thought and in action, in affection and in work, as well as in faith — the two cannot even understand the depth of what it means to be man and woman.

Modern contemporary culture has opened new spaces, new forms of freedom, and new depths in order to enrich the understanding of this difference. But it has also introduced many doubts and much skepticism. For example, I ask myself, if the so-called gender theory is not ... an expression of frustration and resignation, which seeks to cancel out sexual difference because it no longer knows how to confront it. Yes, we risk taking a step backward. The removal of difference in fact creates a problem, not a solution. To resolve the problems in their relationships, men and women need to speak to one another more, listen to each other more, get to know one another better, love one another more. They must treat each other with respect and cooperate in friendship. On this human basis, sustained by the grace of God, it is possible to plan a lifelong marital and familial union. The marital and familial bond is a serious matter, and it is so for everyone, not just for believers. I would urge intellectuals not to leave this theme aside, as if it had to become secondary in order to foster a more free and just society.

God entrusted the earth to the alliance between man and woman: Its failure deprives the earth of warmth and darkens the sky of hope. The signs are already worrisome, and we see them. I would like to indicate, among many others, two points that I believe call for urgent attention.

The first: There is no doubt that we must do far more to advance women if we want to give more strength to the reciprocity between man and woman. In fact, it is necessary that woman not only be listened to more, but that her voice carry real weight, a recognized authority in society and in the Church. [Consider the] way Jesus considered women, in a context less favorable than ours because women in those times were relegated to second place. Jesus considered her in a way which gives off a powerful light, which enlightens a path that leads afar, of which we have only covered a small stretch. We have not yet understood in depth what the feminine genius can give us, what woman can give to society and also to us. Maybe women see things in a way that complements the thoughts of men. It is a path to follow with greater creativity and courage.

A second reflection concerns the topic of man and woman created in the image of God. I wonder if the crisis of collective trust in God, which does us so much harm, and makes us pale with resignation, incredulity, and cynicism, is not also connected to the crisis of the alliance between man and woman. In fact, the biblical account, with the great symbolic fresco depicting the earthly paradise and original sin, tells us in fact that the communion with God is reflected in the communion of the human couple, and the loss of trust in the heavenly Father generates division and conflict between man and woman.

The great responsibility of the Church, of all believers, and first of all of believing families, which derives from us, impels people to rediscover the beauty of the creative design that also inscribes the image of God in the alliance between man and woman. The earth is filled with harmony and trust when the alliance between man and woman is lived properly. And if man and woman seek it together, between themselves, and with God, without a doubt they will find it. Jesus encourages us explicitly to bear witness to this beauty, which is the image of God.

MEN AND WOMEN (II)

I[10] would like to [look at the] narrative ... we find in the second chapter. Here we read that the Lord, after having created heaven and earth, "formed man of dust from the ground, and breathed into his nostrils the breath of life; and man became a living being" (Gn 2:7). This is the culmination of creation. But something is missing: Then God places man in the most beautiful garden that he might cultivate and look after it (see 2:15).

The Holy Spirit, who inspired the whole of the Bible, momentarily evokes the image of man alone — something is missing — without woman. And the Holy Spirit evokes God's thoughts, even his emotion, as he gazes at Adam, observing him alone in the garden. He is free, he is a lord ... but he is alone. And God sees that this "is not good," as if what is missing is communion; he lacks communion, the fullness is lacking. "It is not good," God says, "I will make him a helper fit for him" (2:18).

And so God brings all the animals to man; man gives to each its name — and this is another image of man's dominion over creation — but he sees that not one of the animals is like himself. Man continues alone. When God finally presents woman, man exultantly recognizes that this creature, and this creature alone, is a part of him: "bone of my bones and flesh of my flesh" (2:23). Finally, there is a reflection, a reciprocity. When a person — to give an example to help us understand — wants to shake hands with another, he must have that person before him: If he holds out his hand and no one is there ... his hand remains outstretched, there is no reciprocity. This was how man was, he lacked something to reach his fullness; reciprocity was lacking. Woman is not a replica of man; she comes directly from the creative act of God. The image of the "rib" in no way expresses inferiority or subordination, but, on the contrary, that man and woman are of the same substance and are complimentary, and that they also have this reciprocity. And the fact that — also in that parable — God molds woman while man sleeps means precisely that she is in no way man's creation, but God's. He also suggests another point: In order to find woman — and we could say to find love in woman — man first must dream of her and then find her. God's faith in man and in woman, those to whom he entrusted the earth, is generous, direct, and full. He trusts them. But then the devil introduces suspicion into their minds, disbelief, distrust, and, finally, disobedience to the commandment that protected them. They fall into that delirium of omnipotence that pollutes everything and destroys harmony. We too feel it inside of us, all of us, frequently.

Sin generates distrust and division between man and woman. Their relationship will be undermined by a thousand forms of abuse and subjugation, misleading seduction, and humiliating ignorance, even the most dramatic and violent kind. And history bears the scar. Let us think, for example, of those negative excesses of patriarchal cultures. Think of the many forms of male dominance whereby the woman was considered second-class. Think of the exploitation and the commercialization of the female body in the current media culture. And let us also think of the recent epidemic of distrust, skepticism, and even hostility that is spreading in our culture — in particular an understandable distrust from women — on the part of a covenant between man and woman that is capable, at the same time, of refining the intimacy of communion and of guarding the dignity of difference.

If we do not find a surge of respect for this covenant, capable of protecting new generations from distrust and indifference, children will come into the world ever more uprooted from the mother's womb. The social devaluation for the stable and generative alliance between man and woman is certainly a loss for everyone. We must return marriage and the family to the place of honor! The Bible says something beautiful: Man finds woman, they meet, and man must leave something in order to find her fully. That is why man will leave his father and mother to go to her. It's beautiful! This means setting out on a new path. Man is everything for woman and woman is everything for man.

The responsibility of guarding this covenant between man and woman is ours, although we are sinners and are wounded, confused and humiliated, discouraged and uncertain; it is nevertheless for us believers a demanding and gripping vocation in today's situation. The same narrative of creation and of sin ends by showing us an extremely beautiful icon: "The Lord God made for Adam and for his wife garments of skins, and clothed them" (Gn 3:21). It is an image of tenderness toward the sinful couple that leaves our mouths agape, the tenderness God has for man and woman! It's an image of fatherly care for the human couple. God himself cares for and protects his masterpiece.

THREE EXPRESSIONS

Today's[11] catechesis will serve as a doorway to a series of reflections on family life and what it's really like to live in a family, day in and day out. Imagine three expressions written above the doorway; expressions I've already mentioned here in St. Peter's Square several times before. The expressions are: "May I?", "Thank you," and "Pardon me." Indeed, these expressions open up the way to living well in your family, to living in peace. They are simple expressions, but not so simple to put into practice! They hold much power: the power to keep home life intact even when tested with a thousand problems. But if they are absent, little holes can start to crack open and the whole thing may even collapse.

We usually include these expressions under the general category of being "well-mannered." Okay, a well-mannered person asks permission, says thanks, and asks forgiveness after making a mistake. Very well. But good manners really are that important. A great bishop, Francis de Sales, used to say that "Good manners are already half the way to holiness." But be careful: History has shown that good manners also can become a kind of formalism that masks a dryness of soul and indifference toward the other person. It is often said, "Behind a lot of good manners lurk a lot of bad habits." Not even religion is immune from the risk of having formal observance sink into spiritual worldliness. The Devil, tempting Jesus, boasts of good manners. Indeed, he presents himself as a gentleman, a knight in shining armor. He even presents himself as a theologian by quoting Holy Scripture. He appears to have everything right and neat on the outside, but his intent is always to lead others astray from the truth of God's love. We, however, mean "good manners" only in the most authentic way, according to which the habit of cultivating good relations is firmly rooted in a love for the good and a respect for the other person. The family lives according to this refined sense of loving.

Let's look at these expressions: The first expression is "May I?" When we take care to ask for something kindly — even something we think we have a rightful claim to — we help to strengthen the common life that undergirds marriage and the family. Entering into the life of another, even when that person already has a part to play in our life, demands the sensitivity of a noninvasive attitude which renews trust and respect. Indeed, the deeper and more intimate love is, the more it calls for respect for the other's freedom and the ability to wait until the other opens the door to his or her heart. At this point, we can remember the words of Jesus in the Book of Revelation: "Behold, I stand at the door and knock; if anyone hears my voice and opens the door, I will come in to him and eat with him, and he with me" (3:20). Even the Lord asks permission to enter! Let us not forget that. Before doing anything in your family, ask: "Do you mind if I do this? Would you like me to do this?" This way of asking is well-mannered indeed, but it is also full of love. This does so much good for families.

The second expression is "Thank you." Sometimes we

have to wonder if we are turning into a civilization of bad manners and bad words, as if this were a sign of self-liberation. It's not uncommon to hear these bad words publicly. Kindness and the ability to say "Thank you" are often considered a sign of weakness and raise the suspicion of others. This tendency is encountered even within the nucleus of the family. We must become firmly determined to educate others to be grateful and appreciative: The dignity of the person and social justice must both pass through the portal of the family. If family life neglects this style of living, social life will also reject it. Gratitude, however, stands at the very core of the faith of the believer. A Christian who does not know how to thank has lost the very "language" of God. This is terrible! Let's not forget Jesus' question after he heals the ten lepers and only one of them returns to thank him (see Lk 17:18). I remember once listening to a very wise, old person ... with that uncommon wisdom of life and piety: "Gratitude is a plant that grows only in the soil of noble souls." That nobility of soul, that grace of God in the soul compels us to say "Thank you" with gratitude. It is the flower of a noble soul. This really is something beautiful.

The third expression is "Pardon me." Granted, it's not always easy to say, but it is so necessary. Whenever it is lacking, the little cracks begin to open up — even when we don't want them to — and they can even become enormous sinkholes. It's hardly insignificant that in the Our Father Jesus teaches us — a prayer that sums up all of life's essential questions — we find this expression: "Forgive us our trespasses, as we forgive those who trespass against us" (Mt 6:12). To acknowledge that we have fallen short, to be desirous of returning that which has been taken away — respect, sincerity, love — these make us worthy of pardon. This is how we heal the infection. If we are not able to forgive ourselves, then we are no longer able to forgive period. A house in which the words "I'm sorry" are never uttered begins to lack air, and the flood waters begin to choke those who live inside. So many wounds, so many scrapes and bruises are the result of a lack of these precious words: "I am sorry." Marital life is so often torn apart by fights ... the "plates will even start flying," but let me give you a word of advice: Never finish the day without making peace with one another. Listen to me carefully: Did you fight with your wife or husband? Kids — did you fight with your parents? Did you seriously argue? That's not a good thing, but it's not really that which is the problem: The problem arises only if this feeling hangs over into the next day. So, if you've fought, do not let the day end without making peace with your family. And how am I going to make peace? By getting down on my knees? No! Just by a small gesture, a little something, and harmony within your family will be restored. Just a little caress, no words necessary. But don't let the sun go down on your family without having made your peace. Do you understand me? It's not easy, but you have to do it. It will help to make life so much more beautiful.

FAMILIES AND POVERTY
So[12] many problems are testing families.

One of these trials is poverty. Let us think of the many families that live on the outskirts of major cities, as well as those in rural areas. ... So much misery, so much degradation! And then, to make the situation worse, in some places there is also war. War is always a terrible thing. Moreover, it also strikes above all the civil populations, the families. Truly, war is the "mother of all poverty," war impoverishes the family, a great predator of lives, souls, and of the most sacred and beloved bonds.

Despite all this, there are many poor families who try to live their daily lives with dignity, often openly entrusting themselves to God's blessing. This lesson, however, should not justify our indifference, but rather increase our shame over the fact that there is so much poverty! It is almost a miracle that, even in poverty, the family continues to form, and even preserve — as much as it can — the special humanity of those bonds. This fact irritates those planners of well-being who consider attachments, procreation, and familial bonds as secondary variables to the quality of life. They don't understand a thing! On the contrary, we should kneel down before these families, who are a true school of humanity in saving societies from barbarity.

What do we have left if we yield to the extortion of Caesar and Mammon, to violence and to money, and renounce even family ties? A new civil ethic will arrive only when the leaders of public life reorganize the social bond beginning with the perverse struggle that spirals between the family and poverty, which leads us into the abyss.

The prevailing economy is often concentrated on the enjoyment of individual well-being, but it largely exploits family ties. This is a serious contradiction! The boundless work of the family is not quoted in financial statements, obviously. Indeed, economics and politics are misers in regard to acknowledging this. Yet, the interior formation of the person and the social flow of affections have their mainstay precisely there. Should it be removed, everything would fall apart.

It is not merely a question of bread. We are talking about work, talking about education, talking about health. It is important that this be clearly understood. We are always quite moved when we see images of sick and malnourished children that are shown in so many parts of the world. At the same time, we are also deeply moved by the twinkle in the eyes of many children, deprived of everything and in schools built from nothing, who are proud when showing off their pencil and their notebook. And how lovingly they look at their teacher. Children already know that man does not live on bread alone! And as for family affection; when there is destitution, children suffer because they want love, family ties.

We Christians have to be ever closer to the families whom poverty puts to the test. But think, all of you know someone: a father without work, a mother without work ... and this makes the family suffer, the bonds are weakened. This is terrible. Indeed, social destitution strikes the family and sometimes destroys it. The lack, loss, or strong instability of employment weigh heavily upon family life, imposing a substantial strain on relationships. Living conditions in the poorest neighborhoods, with housing and transportation problems, as well as reduced social, health, and educational services, bring about further difficulties. Adding to these material factors is the damage caused to the family by the pseudo-models spread by the mass media on the basis of consumerism and the cult of appearances, which influence the poorest social classes and increase the breakdown of family ties. Take care of families, attend to the attachment, when destitution puts the family to the test!

The Church is mother and must not forget this drama of her children. She too must be poor, to become fruitful and respond to so much poverty. A poor Church is a Church that practices voluntary simplicity in her life — in her very institutions, in the lifestyle of her members — to break down every dividing wall, especially to the poor. Prayer and action are needed. Let us pray earnestly that the Lord stir us, to render our Christian families leaders of this revolution of familial proximity, which is now so essential for us! The Church is made of it, of this familial proximity. Let us not forget that the judgment of the needy, of the small, and of the poor prefigures the judgment of God (see Mt 25:31–46). Let's not forget this and let's do all we can to help families to go forward in the trial of poverty and destitution which strikes attachments and family bonds. I would like to read once again the Bible text that we heard at the beginning, and each of us think about the families who are tried by destitution and poverty, the Bible reads like this: "My son, deprive not the poor of his living, / and do not keep needy eyes waiting. / Do not grieve the one who is hungry, / nor anger a man in want. / Do not add to the troubles of an angry mind, / nor delay your gift to a beggar. / Do not reject an afflicted suppliant, / nor turn your face away from the poor. / Do not avert your eye from the needy, / nor give a man occasion to curse you" (Sir 4:1–5). For this is what the Lord will do — so it says in the Gospel — if we do not do these things.

FAMILIES AND ILLNESS

Within[13] the realm of family bonds, the illness of our loved ones is endured with an "excess" of suffering and anguish. It is love that makes us feel this "excess." So often for a father or a mother it is more difficult to bear a son or daughter's pain than one's own. The family, we can say, has always been the nearest "hospital." Still today, in so many parts of the world, a hospital is for the privileged few, and is often far away. It is the mother, the father, brothers, sisters, and grandparents who guarantee care and help one to heal.

In the Gospels, many pages tell of Jesus' encounters with the sick and of his commitment to healing them. He presents himself publicly as one who fights against illness and who has come to heal mankind of every evil: evils of the spirit and evils of the body. The Gospel scene just referenced from the Gospel According to Mark is truly moving. It says, "That evening, at sundown, they brought to him all who were sick or possessed with demons" (1:32). When I think of today's great cities, I wonder where are the doors to which the sick are brought hoping to be healed! Jesus never held back from their care. He never passed by, never turned his face away. When a father or mother, or even just friends, brought a sick person for him to touch and heal, he never let time be an issue; healing came before the law, even one as sacred as resting on the Sabbath (see Mk 3:1-6). The doctors of the law reproached Jesus because he healed on the Sabbath, he did good on the Sabbath. But the love of Jesus was in giving health, doing good: This always takes priority! ...

In the face of illness, even in families, difficulties arise due to human weakness. But in general, times of illness enable family bonds to grow stronger. I think about how important it is to teach children, starting from childhood, about solidarity in times of illness. An education which protects against sensitivity for human illness withers the heart. It allows young people to be "anaesthetized" against the suffering of others, incapable of facing suffering and of living the experience of limitation. How often do we see a man or woman arrive at work with a weary face, with a tired countenance, and, when we ask them "What happened?" they answer, "I only slept two hours because we are taking turns at home to be close to our boy, our girl, our sick one, our grandfather, our grandmother." And the day of work goes on. These are heroic deeds, the heroism of families! That hidden heroism carried out with tenderness and courage when someone at home is sick.

The weakness and suffering of our dearest and most cherished loved ones can be, for our children and grandchildren, a school of life — it's important to teach the children, the grandchildren to understand this closeness in illness at home — and they become so when times of illness are accompanied by prayer and the affectionate and thoughtful closeness of relatives. The Christian community really knows that the family, in the trial of illness, should not be left on its own. We must say "Thank you" to the Lord for those beautiful experiences of ecclesial fraternity that help families get through the difficult moments of pain and suffering. This Christian closeness, from family to family, is a real treasure for the parish, a treasure of wisdom, which helps families in the difficult moments to understand the kingdom of God better than many discourses! They are God's caresses.

GRIEVING

Death[14] is an experience which touches all families, without exception. It is part of life; yet, where familial love is concerned, death never seems natural. For parents, surviving their own children is particularly heartbreaking; it contradicts the fundamental nature of the very relationships that give meaning to the family. The loss of a son or daughter is like time stopping altogether: It opens a chasm that swallows both past and future. Death, which takes away a little child or young person, is a blow to the promises, to the gifts and the sacrifices of love joyfully brought to the life we gave birth to. Frequently parents come to Mass at Santa Marta with the photo of a son, a daughter, a baby, a boy, a girl, and they say to me, "He's gone, she's gone." And their faces are filled with grief. Death touches us, and when it is a child's, it touches us profoundly. The whole family is left paralyzed, speechless. And the child left alone by the loss of one or both parents suffers in a similar way. She asks: "Where is my daddy? Where is my mama?" — "Well, she is in heaven" — "Why can't I see her?" This question covers the agony in the heart of a child left alone. The emptiness of abandonment that opens up in him is made all the more agonizing by the fact that he doesn't have the life experience to even "give a name" to what has happened. "When is daddy coming back?" "When is mama coming?" What do you say when a child suffers? This is what death in the family is like.

In these cases, death is like a black hole that opens up in the life of the family and for which we have no explanation. And at times we even go so far as to lay the blame on God. How many people — I understand them — get angry with God, blaspheme: "Why did you take my son, my daughter? There is no God, God does not exist! Why did he do this?"

We hear this so often. But this anger is basically what comes from the heart in great pain; the loss of a son or of a daughter, of a father or of a mother, is a great sorrow. This happens over and over in families. In these cases, I said, death is like a hole. But physical death has "accomplices" even worse than itself, which are called hate, envy, pride, greed — in short, the sin of the world which works for death and makes it even more painful and unjust. Family bonds seem to be the predestined and helpless victims of these helping powers of death, trailing the history of mankind. Let us think of the absurd "normality" with which, at certain moments and in certain places, events adding to the horror of death are provoked by the hatred and indifference of other human beings. May the Lord keep us free from being accustomed to this!

In the People of God, by the grace of his compassion granted in Jesus, many families prove by their deeds that death does not have the last word: This is a true act of faith. Every time a family in mourning — even terrible mourning — finds the strength to guard the faith and love that unite us to those we love; it has already prevented death from taking everything. The darkness of death should be confronted with a more intense work of love. "My God, lighten my darkness!" is the invocation of evening prayer. In the light of the resurrection of the Lord, who abandons none of those whom the Father entrusted to him, we can take the "sting" out of death, as the apostle Paul says (see 1 Cor 15:55); we can prevent it from poisoning life, from rendering vain our love, from pushing us into the darkest chasm.

In this faith, we can console one another, knowing that the Lord has conquered death once and for all. Our loved ones are not lost in the darkness of nothing: Hope assures us that they are in the good and strong hands of God. Love is stronger than death. Thus, the way is to let love grow, make it stronger, and love will guard us until the day that every tear shall be wiped away, when "death shall be no more, neither shall there be mourning nor crying nor pain any more" (Rv 21:4). If we allow ourselves to be sustained by this faith, the experience of grief can generate even stronger family bonds, a new openness to the pain of other families, a new brotherhood with families that are born and reborn in hope. To be born and reborn in hope, this gives us faith. But I would like to stress the last phrase of the Gospel which we heard today (see Lk 7:11–15). After Jesus brought the young man, the only son of a widow, back to life, the Gospel says, "Jesus gave him back to his mother." And this is our hope! All our loved ones who are gone, the Lord will give them back to us and we will be together with them. This hope does not disappoint! Let us remember well this action of Jesus: "And Jesus gave him back to his mother," thus the Lord will do with all our loved ones in the family!

This faith protects us from the nihilist vision of death, as well as from the false consolations of the world, so that the Christian truth "does not risk mixing itself with myths of various types," surrendering to superstitious beliefs.[15] Today it is necessary that pastors and all Christians express in a more concrete way the meaning of the Faith in regard to the family experience of grief. We should not deny them the right to weep — we must weep in mourning — "Jesus wept" and was "deeply troubled" by the grave loss of a family that he loved (see Jn 11:33–37). We can draw from the simple and strong testimony of the many families who have been able to grasp, in the most arduous transition of death, the safe passage of the Lord, crucified and risen, with his irrevocable promise of the resurrection of the dead. God's work of love is stronger than the work of death. It is of that love, it is precisely of that love, that we must make ourselves hardworking "accomplices" with our faith! And let us remember Jesus' deed: "And Jesus gave him back to his mother," so he will do with all our loved ones and with us when we meet again, when death will be definitively conquered in us. It was conquered by Jesus' cross. Jesus will give us all back to the family!

WOUNDS

We[16] will reflect on the hurts that are incurred in family life. When, that is, we hurt one another within the family. The worst thing!

We know that in every family history there are moments in which the intimacy of loved ones is offended by the behavior of its members. Words and actions (and omissions!) that, rather than expressing love, dismiss it or even mortify it. When these hurts, which are still rectifiable, are ignored, they deepen: They transform into impertinence, hostility, and contempt. And at that point they can become deep wounds that divide husband and wife, and induce them to find understanding, support, consolation elsewhere. But often these "supports" do not consider the good of the family!

The depletion of conjugal love spreads resentment in relationships. And often this disintegration "collapses" onto the children.

There: the children. I would like to meditate a little on

this point. Despite our seemingly evolved sensitivity, and all our refined psychological analyses, I ask myself if we are not just anaesthetizing ourselves to the wounds in children's souls. The more you try to compensate with gifts and snacks, the more you lose your sense of these spiritual wounds — so painful and so deep. We talk a lot about behavioral problems, mental health, the well-being of the child, about the anxiety of parents and their children. ... But do we even know what a spiritual wound is? Do we feel the weight of the mountain that crushes the soul of a child in those families where members mistreat and hurt one another to the point of breaking the bonds of marital fidelity? How much weight do our choices have — mistaken choices, for example — how much weight do they place on the soul of our children? When adults lose their head, when each one thinks only of himself or herself, when a dad and mom hurt one another, the souls of their children suffer terribly, they experience a sense of despair. And these wounds leave a mark that lasts their whole lives.

In the family, everything is connected: When her soul is wounded in some way, the infection spreads to everyone. And when a man and a woman, who have committed to being "one flesh" and forming a family, think obsessively of their own need for freedom and gratification, this bias affects the hearts and lives of their children in a profound way. Frequently these children hide to cry alone. ... We need to understand this fully. Husband and wife are one flesh. Their own little children are flesh of their flesh. If we think of the harshness with which Jesus admonishes adults not to scandalize the little ones — we heard the Gospel passage (see Mt 18:6) — we can also better understand his words on the serious responsibility to guard the marital bond that gives rise to the human family (19:6–9). When man and woman have become one flesh, all the father-and-mother's wounds and neglect have an impact on the living flesh of their children.

It is true, on the other hand, that there are cases in which separation is inevitable. At times it becomes even morally necessary, precisely when it is a matter of removing the weaker spouse or young children from the gravest wounds caused by abuse and violence, by humiliation and exploitation, by disregard and indifference.

There are, thanks be to God, those who, sustained by faith and by love for their children, bear witness to their fidelity to a bond they believed in, although it may seem impossible to revive it. Not all those who are separated feel called to this vocation. Not all discern, in their solitude, the Lord calling them. Around us we find various families in so-called irregular situations — I don't really like this word — and it causes us to wonder. How do we help them? How do we accompany them? How do we accompany them so that the children aren't taken hostage by either dad or mom?

Let us ask the Lord for great faith in order to see reality through the eyes of God; and for great charity in order to approach people with his merciful heart.

ENEMIES OF UNITY

WHERE THERE ARE LIES, THERE IS NO LOVE

To[1] live with false communication is serious because it impedes relationships and, therefore, impedes love. Where there are lies there is no love; there can be no love. And when we speak about interpersonal communication, we do not mean words alone, but also gestures, attitudes, even silence and absence. A person speaks with all that he is and does. We are always communicating. We all live by communicating, and we are always poised between truth and lies.

But what does it mean to tell the truth? Does it mean being sincere? Or precise? In fact, this is not enough, because one can be genuinely mistaken, or one can be precise in the details but not grasp the overall sense. At times we justify ourselves by saying, "But I said what I felt!" Yes, but you have presented your point of view as an absolute. Or, "I only told the truth!" Perhaps, but you revealed personal or private matters. How much gossip destroys communion by inopportune comments or lack of sensitivity. Indeed, gossip kills, and James the Apostle said this in his letter. Those who gossip are people who kill: They kill others because the tongue kills as much as a knife. Be careful.

FALSEHOOD IS NEVER HARMLESS

There[2] is no such thing as harmless disinformation; on the contrary, trusting in falsehood can have dire consequences. Even a seemingly slight distortion of the truth can have dangerous effects. ... The most radical antidote to the virus of falsehood is purification by the truth. In Christianity, truth is not just a conceptual reality that regards how we judge things, defining them as true or false. The truth is not just bringing to light things that are concealed, "revealing reality," as the ancient Greek term *aletheia* (from *a-lethès*, "not hidden") might lead us to believe. Truth involves our whole life. In the Bible, it carries with it the sense of support, solidity, and trust, as implied by the root *'aman*, the source of our liturgical expression "Amen." Truth is something you can lean on, so as not to fall. In this relational sense, the only truly reliable and trustworthy One — the One on whom we can count — is the living God. ... The best antidotes to falsehoods are not strategies but people: people who are not greedy but ready to listen; people who make the effort to engage in sincere dialogue so that the truth can emerge; people who are attracted by goodness and take responsibility for how they use language.

GOSSIP

Communication[3] is not just the transmission of news: It is availability, mutual enrichment, relationship. Unfortunately, a form of communication that continues to be widespread has nothing to do with attention to one another and with mutual understanding: It is gossip. It is a bad habit that every day undermines the human community, sowing envy, jealousy, and lust for power. You can even kill a person with this weapon, either by striking with it, or rather creating gossip, or by passing it on, when hearing it, prolonging life to lies and anonymous tip-offs. It is important, therefore, to communicate responsibly, also thinking about the harm you can do with language, with chatter, with gossip.

LACK OF OPENNESS TO DIALOGUE

Our[4] defensiveness is evident when we are entrenched within our ideas and our own strengths — in which case we slip into Pelagianism — or when we are ambitious or vain. These defensive mechanisms prevent us from truly understanding other people and from opening ourselves to a sincere dialogue with them. But the Church, flowing from Pentecost, is given the fire of the Holy Spirit, which does not so much fill the mind with ideas but enflames the heart; she is moved by the breath of the Spirit which does not transmit a power, but rather an ability to serve in love, a language which everyone is able to understand.

THE WALLS THAT BLOCK RECONCILIATION

Dialogue[5] is carried out with humility, even at the cost of "swallowing bitter pills," because we must not allow "walls" of resentment and hatred to grow in our hearts. ... In order to open up dialogue, not much time must pass. In fact, problems must be tackled as soon as possible. We must immediately approach dialogue, because time makes the wall rise up like the weeds that block the growth of wheat. And when walls rise up, reconciliation is so difficult! In our hearts there is the possibility of becoming like Berlin, with a wall raised against others.

THE LOGIC OF REPAYMENT IS NOT CHRISTIAN

Jesus[6] ... says, "When you give a feast, invite the poor, the maimed, the lame, the blind, and you will be blessed, because they cannot repay you" (Lk 14:13–14). Here, too, Jesus goes completely against the tide, manifesting as always the logic of God the Father. And he also adds the key by which to interpret this discourse of his. And what is the key? A promise: If you do this, you "will be repaid at the resurrection of the just" (14:14). This means that those who behave in this way will receive divine compensation, far superior to human repayment: I do this favor for you expecting you to do one for me. No, this is not Christian. Humble generosity is Christian. Indeed, human repayment usually distorts relationships, making them "commercial" by bringing personal interest into a relationship that should be generous and free. Instead, Jesus encourages selfless generosity, to pave our way toward a much greater joy, the joy of partaking in the very love of God who awaits us, all of us, at the heavenly banquet.

SPIRITUAL INDIVIDUALISM

[In prayer] I urge you[7] to "avoid the risk of an individualistic approach, and remember that God's word is given to us precisely to build communion, to unite us in the Truth along our path to God. ... Consequently, the sacred text must always be approached in the communion of the Church" (*Verbum Domini*, 86).

OVERCOME BY COMFORT AND SELFISHNESS

The[8] content of Christian witness is not a theory, it's not an ideology or a complex system of precepts and prohibitions or a moralist theory, but a message of salvation, a real event, rather, a Person: It is the Risen Christ, the living and only Savior of all. He can be testified to by those who have personal experience of him, in prayer and in the Church, through a journey that has its foundation in baptism, its nourishment in the Eucharist, its seal in confirmation, its continual conversion in penitence. Thanks to this journey, ever guided by the Word of God, every Christian can become a witness of the risen Jesus. And his/her witness is all the more credible the more it shines through a life lived by the Gospel, a joyful, courageous, gentle, peaceful, merciful life. Instead, if a Christian gives in to ease, vanity, selfishness, if he or she becomes deaf and blind to the question of "resurrection" of many brothers and sisters, how can he/she communicate the living Jesus, how can the Christian communicate the freeing power of the living Jesus and his infinite tenderness?

BETRAYAL OF OUR HUMANITY

Each of us[9] has been created to love and care for others, and this culminates in the gift of self: "Greater love has no man than this, that a man lay down his life for his friends" (Jn 15:13). In the relationship we establish with others we risk our humanity, coming closer to or moving away from the model of the human being willed by God the Father and revealed in the Incarnate Son. Therefore, any choice contrary to the accomplishment of God's plan for us is a betrayal of our humanity and a renunciation of the "life in abundance" offered by Jesus Christ. It means descending, lowering ourselves, becoming animals.

IF TECHNOLOGY BECOMES A BARRIER TO ENCOUNTER

True[10] wisdom, as the fruit of self-examination, dialogue, and generous encounter between persons, is not acquired by a mere accumulation of data which eventually leads to overload and confusion, a sort of mental pollution. Real relationships with others, with all the challenges they entail, now tend to be replaced by a type of internet communication which enables us to choose or eliminate relationships at a whim, thus giving rise to a new type of contrived emotion which has more to do with devices and displays than with other people and with nature. Today's media do enable us to communicate and to share our knowledge and affections. Yet at times they also shield us from direct contact with the pain, the fears and joys of others, and the complexity of their personal experiences. For this reason, we should be concerned that, alongside the exciting possibilities offered by these media, a deep and melancholic dissatisfaction with interpersonal relations, or a harmful sense of isolation, can also arise.

THE CELL PHONE AS DRUG

Cell phones[11] are a great help, a great step forward. They should be used. It's great that everyone knows how to use them. But when you become a slave to your cell phone, you lose your freedom. The cell phone is for communicating, for communication. It is so wonderful to communicate with each other. But be careful, there is a danger that when the cell phone is a drug, then communication is reduced to "contact." Life is not for "contacting each other," it is for communicating! Let us remember what St. Augustine wrote: *"in interiore homine habitat veritas"* (*De vera religione*, 39, 72): "Truth dwells within the depths of the person." We must seek it. This is true for everyone, for those who believe and for those who do not believe. We all have depths. Only in inner silence can we hear the voice of conscience and distinguish it from the voices of selfishness and hedonism, which are different voices.

THE RISKS OF VIRTUAL SPACES

Social[12] networks, too, especially for young people, are a seemingly endless opportunity for encounter: The internet can offer more opportunities for encounter and solidarity among all, and this is a good thing; it is a gift of God. However, for every instrument that is offered to us, the choice that mankind decides to make of it is fundamental. The communicative environment can help us to grow or, on the contrary, to become disoriented. The risks inherent in some of these virtual spaces must not be underestimated; through the web, many young people are lured and drawn into slavery from which it then becomes beyond their ability to free themselves. In this sphere, adults, parents, and teachers — also older siblings and cousins — are called to the task of watching over and protecting youths. You must do the same with your relatives and friends: perceive and point out particular vulnerabilities, suspicious cases on which light must be shed.

Thus use the web to share a positive account of your experiences of encounter with our brothers and sisters in the world, recount and share good practices and generate a virtuous circle.

CONNECTED YET ALONE

It[13] is paradoxical that while [people] are immersed in a vortex of communication, and through social media they can feel they are citizens of the world, they nonetheless experience deep dissatisfaction and loneliness. While they connect with everything and everyone, they seem to lack the ability to place themselves with full awareness in the course of history and to look forward and trust the future. If the task of guiding and training has always characterized the mission of the universities, today it seems even more necessary that the academic and cultural institutions should know how to offer young people the tools to inhabit history by treasuring the enormous wealth of knowledge and wisdom inherited from the past. It is only from this legacy that the future of humanity can be built in a truly innovative way, enhancing the progress of science and technology within an integral vision of the human person made in the image and likeness of God.

LOVE WITHOUT TRUTH

Only[14] to the extent that love is grounded in truth can it endure over time, can it transcend the passing moment and be sufficiently solid to sustain a shared journey. If love is not tied to truth, it falls prey to fickle emotions and cannot stand the test of time. True love, on the other hand, unifies all the elements of our person and becomes a new light pointing the way to a great and fulfilled life. Without truth, love is incapable of establishing a firm bond; it cannot liberate our isolated ego or redeem it from the fleeting moment in order to create life and bear fruit.

AN IMPOSED TRUTH

The[15] light of love proper to faith can illumine the questions of our own time about truth. Truth nowadays is often reduced to the subjective authenticity of the individual, valid only for the life of the individual. A common truth intimidates us, for we identify it with the intransigent demands of totalitarian systems. But if truth is a truth of love, if it is a truth disclosed in personal encounter with the Other and with others, then it can be set free from its enclosure in individuals and become part of the common good. As a truth of love, it is not one that can be imposed by force; it is not a truth that stifles the individual. Since it is born of love, it can penetrate to the heart, to the personal core of each man and woman. Clearly, then, faith is not intransigent, but grows in respectful coexistence with others. One who believes may not be presumptuous; on the contrary, truth leads to humility, since believers know that, rather than ourselves possessing truth, it is truth which embraces and possesses us. Far from making us inflexible, the security of faith sets us on a journey; it enables witness and dialogue with all.

SEPARATING COMMUNICATION FROM REALITY

I don't know[16] what the communication of the future will be like. I think of what communication was like, for example, when I was a boy, without a TV yet, with the radio, with the newspaper, even the clandestine newspaper that was persecuted by whatever government was in power, sold at night by volunteers ... and oral communication. If we compare it to this, it was precarious information, and today's communication will perhaps be precarious compared to the future. What remains as a constant of communication is the ability to convey a fact and to distinguish it from the narrative, from what is reported. One of the things that damages communication — past, present, and future — is hearsay. There is a very nice study, released three years ago, by Simone Paganini, a scholar at the University of Aachen in Germany, and it talks about the movement of communication between the writer, the written, and the reader. There is always the risk of communication moving from the fact to the narrative, and this ruins the communication. It is important to keep the fact and always approach the fact. I see this in the Curia as well: There is a fact, and then each person embellishes it by putting his own spin on it, without ill intent — this is the dynamic. So, the asceticism of the communicator is always to return to the fact, report the fact, and then say, "This is my interpretation, I was told this," distinguishing the fact from hearsay. Some time ago I was told the story of Little Red Riding Hood, but based on what was reported, and it ended with Little Red Riding Hood and the grandmother putting the wolf in the pot and eating him! The storytelling changed things. Whatever the medium, the guarantee is fidelity. Can hearsay be used? Yes, it can be used in communication, but always be on the alert to ascertain the objectivity of the hearsay. This is one of the values that must be pursued in communication. Second, communication must be human, and by human I mean constructive — that is, it must make the other person grow. Communication cannot be used as a weapon because it is anti-human, it destroys. A little while ago ... I found [an article] in a magazine entitled "Words Can Be Like Tiny Doses of Arsenic." Communication must be at the service of construction, not destruction. And when does communication serve destruction? When it defends nonhuman projects. Think of the propaganda of the dictatorships of the past century. They knew how to communicate well, but they fomented war, division, and destruction.

JOURNEYING IN FAITH AND MUTUAL LOVE

CARRYING THE GOSPEL INTO EVERY SETTING

Every[1] encounter with Christ, who in the sacraments gives us salvation, invites us to "go" and communicate to others the salvation that we have been able to see, to touch, to encounter, and to receive, and which is truly credible because it is love. In this way, the sacraments spur us to be missionaries, and the apostolic commitment to carry the Gospel into every setting, including those most hostile, is the most authentic fruit of an assiduous sacramental life, since it is a participation in the saving initiative of God, who desires salvation for all people.

SELF-GIVING

Effective[2] Christian witness is not about bombarding people with religious messages, but about our willingness to be available to others "by patiently and respectfully engaging their questions and their doubts as they advance in their search for the truth and the meaning of human existence."[3] We need but recall the story of the disciples on the way to Emmaus. We have to be able to dialogue with the men and women of today, to understand their expectations, doubts and hopes, and to bring them the Gospel, Jesus Christ himself, God incarnate, who died and rose to free us from sin and death. We are challenged to be people of depth, attentive to what is happening around us and spiritually alert. To dialogue means to believe that the "other" has something worthwhile to say, and to entertain his or her point of view and perspective. Engaging in dialogue does not mean renouncing our own ideas and traditions, but the claim that they alone are valid or absolute.

May the image of the Good Samaritan who tended to the wounds of the injured man by pouring oil and wine over them be our inspiration. Let our communication be a balm which relieves pain and a fine wine which gladdens hearts. May the light we bring to others not be the result of cosmetics or special effects, but rather of our being loving and merciful "neighbors" to those wounded and left on the side of the road. Let us boldly become citizens of the digital world. The Church needs to be concerned for, and present in, the world of communication in order to dialogue with people today and to help them encounter Christ. She needs to be a Church at the side of others, capable of accompanying everyone along the way. The revolution taking place in communications media and in information technologies represents a great and thrilling challenge; may we respond to that challenge with fresh energy and imagination as we seek to share with others the beauty of God.

THE JOY OF RESURRECTION ON OUR FACES

To[4] all and to each, therefore, let us not tire of saying: Christ is risen! Let us repeat it all together, today here in [St. Peter's] Square: Christ is risen! Let us repeat it with words, but above all with the witness of our lives. The happy news of the Resurrection should shine on our faces, in our feelings and attitudes, in the way we treat others.

OFFERING HOPE

Digital[5] communication offers a number of possibilities, the most important of which is the proclamation of the Gospel. Certainly, though important, acquiring technical knowledge is not enough. First, it means encountering real women and men, who are often wounded or lost, in order to give them real reasons to hope. Proclamation requires authentic human relationships destined to culminate in a personal encounter with the Lord. Therefore, the internet is not enough, technology does not suffice. This, however, does not mean that the Church's presence online is useless; on the contrary, her presence is indispensable, always with an evangelical style, in what for many, specifically young people, has become a kind of life environment, to stir up in hearts the insuppressible questions about the meaning of life and to point to the way that leads to him who is the answer: Divine Mercy made flesh, the Lord Jesus.

SIMPLE FRATERNAL GESTURES

We must[6] listen to the word of the Lord, to what he says to us. But we must also listen to how he says it. And we must do as he does ... but do it as he says it: with love, with tenderness, with that "self-humbling" toward our brothers and sisters.

To[7] those who, today too, "wish to see Jesus;" to those who are searching for the face of God; to those who received catechesis when they were little and then developed it no further and perhaps have lost their faith; to so many who have not yet encountered Jesus personally; ... to all these people we can offer three things: the Gospel, the crucifix, and the witness of our faith, poor but sincere. The Gospel: There we can encounter Jesus, listen to him, know him. The crucifix: the sign of the love of Jesus who gave himself for us. And then a faith that is expressed in simple gestures of fraternal charity. But mainly in the coherence of life, between what we say and what we do.

The[8] Gospel of John tells us that "the truth will make you free" (8:32). The truth is ultimately Christ himself, whose gentle mercy is the yardstick for measuring the way we proclaim the truth and condemn injustice. Our primary task is to uphold the truth with love (see Eph 4:15). Only words spoken with love and accompanied by meekness and mercy can touch our sinful hearts. Harsh and moralistic words and actions risk further alienating those whom we wish to lead to conversion and freedom, reinforcing their sense of rejection and defensiveness.

What we say and how we say it, every word and every gesture, should be able to express God's compassion, tenderness, and forgiveness for all. Love, by its nature, is communication. It leads to openness and not isolation. And if our hearts and gestures are animated by charity, by divine love, our communication will bring God's strength.

TRUTH WITH GOODNESS AND BEAUTY

And[9] our communication must be witness. If you want to communicate just one truth without goodness and beauty, stop, do not do it. If you want to communicate a truth, but without involving yourselves, without witnessing that truth with your own life, with your own flesh, stop, do not do it. There is always the signature of the witness in each of the things we do. Witnesses. ... We have fallen into the culture of adjectives and adverbs, and we have forgotten the strength of nouns. The communicator must make people understand the weight of the reality of nouns that reflect the reality of people. And this is a mission of communication: to communicate with reality, without sweetening with adjectives or adverbs. ... "How, do you know that person?" — "Ah, that person is like this, like that ...": immediately the adjective. First the adjective, perhaps then, afterward, what the person is like. This culture of the adjective has entered the Church, and we, all brothers, forget to be brothers, by saying that this is "this type of" brother, that one is "the other" brother: first the adjective. Your communication should be austere but beautiful: Beauty is not rococo art, beauty does not need these rococo things; beauty manifests itself from the noun itself, without strawberries on the cake! I think we need to learn this.

Communicating by witness, communicating by involving oneself in communication, communicating with the nouns of things, communicating as martyrs — that is, as witnesses of Christ, as martyrs — to learn the language of the martyrs, which is the language of the apostles.

THE GOSPEL DECENTERS US

Following[10] Jesus entails giving up evil and selfishness and choosing good, truth, and justice, even when this demands sacrifice and the renunciation of our own interests. And this indeed divides; as we know, it even cuts the closest ties. However, be careful: It is not Jesus who creates division! He establishes the criterion: whether to live for ourselves or to live for God and for others; to be served or to serve; to obey one's own ego or to obey God. It is in this sense that Jesus is a "sign that is spoken against" (Lk 2:34). ... The Christian's real force is the force of truth and of love. Starting[11] anew with Christ means imitating him by leaving ourselves behind and going out to encounter others. This is a beautiful experience, and yet a paradox. Why? Because when we put Christ at the center of our life, we ourselves don't become the center! The more that you unite yourself to Christ and he becomes the center of your life, the more he leads you out of yourself, leads you from making yourself the center and opens you to others. This is the true dynamism of love, this is the movement of God himself! God is the center, but he is always self-gift, relationship, love that gives itself away ... and this is what we will become if we remain united to Christ. He will draw us into this dynamism of love. Where there is true life in Christ, there follows an openness to others, and [therefore] a going out from oneself to encounter others in the name of Christ. And this is the job of the catechist: constantly to go forth to others out of love, to bear witness to Jesus, and to talk about Jesus, to proclaim Jesus. This is important because the Lord does it: It is the Lord himself who impels us to go forth. The[12] Word of God arouses amazement in us. It has the power to astonish us. The Gospel is the word of life: It does not oppress people; on the contrary, it frees those who are slaves to the many evil spirits of this world: the spirit of vanity, attachment to money, pride, sensuality. ... The Gospel changes the heart, changes life, transforms evil inclinations into good intentions. The Gospel is capable of changing people! Therefore, it is the task of Christians to spread the redeeming power throughout the world, becoming missionaries and heralds of the Word of God.

FAITH RENEWS OUR GAZE ON REALITY

Faith[13] engages us in action and gives rise to good habits. It is a gaze that accompanies processes, transforms problems into opportunities, improves and builds the city of man. I wish you to always know how to refine and defend this gaze, to overcome the temptation not to see, to distance or exclude. And I encourage you not to discriminate, not to consider anyone as surplus, not to settle for what everyone sees. Let no one dictate your agenda except the poor, the least, the suffering. Do not swell the ranks of those who rush to tell the story of that part of reality that is already illuminated by the world's spotlight. Start from the outskirts, aware that they are not the end, but the beginning of the city. ... Don't be afraid to get involved. Words — true words — carry weight. They are sustained only by those who incarnate them in life. Witnessing, moreover, contributes to your own trustworthiness: passionate and joyful witnessing. This is my concluding wish for you, again making the words of St. Paul VI my own:

> Love for the cause is needed. If we do not love this cause, we will accomplish little, we will tire of it immediately, we will see its difficulties, we will also see its inconveniences, controversies, debts. ... We must have a great love for the cause, we must say that we believe in what we are doing and what we want to do.[14]

ECCLESIAL COMMUNION

CHRIST UNITES US IN LOVE

By[1] giving us this new commandment, he asks us to love one another, not only and not so much with our love, but with his, which the Holy Spirit instills in our hearts if we invoke him with faith. In this way — and only in this way — can we love one another not only as we love ourselves but as he loved us — that is, infinitely more. Indeed, God loves us much more than we love ourselves. And thus we can spread everywhere the seed of love that renews relationships between people and opens horizons of hope. Jesus always opens horizons of hope. His love opens horizons of hope. This love makes us become new men, brothers and sisters in the Lord, and makes us the new People of God, which is the Church, in which everyone is called to love Christ and to love one another in him. ...

Jesus' love shows us the other as a present or future member of the community of Jesus' friends. It spurs us to dialogue and helps us to listen to one another and to mutually get to know each other. Love opens up toward the other, becoming the foundation of human relationships. It renders us capable of overcoming the barriers of our own weaknesses and prejudices. Jesus' love within us creates bridges, teaches new paths, triggers the dynamism of fraternity.

There[2] is a dynamism of solidarity which builds up the Church as the family of God, for whom the experience of *koinonia* is central. What does this strange word mean? It is a Greek word which means "pooling one's goods," "sharing in common," being a community, not isolated. This is the experience of the first Christian community — that is, "communality," "sharing," "communicating, participating," not isolation. In the primitive Church, this *koinonia*, this communality, refers primarily to participation in the Body and Blood of Christ. This is why, when we receive holy Communion, we say that "we communicate," we enter into communion with Jesus, and from this communion with Jesus we reach a communion with our brothers and sisters. And this communion in the Body and Blood of Christ that we share during holy Mass translates into fraternal union and, therefore, also into what is most difficult for us, pooling our resources and collecting money for the mother Church in Jerusalem (see Rom 12:13; 2 Cor 8–9) and the other churches.

If you want to know whether you are good Christians, you have to pray, try to draw near to Communion, to the Sacrament of Reconciliation. But the sign that your heart has converted is when conversion reaches the pocket, when it touches one's own interests. That is when one can see whether one is generous to others, if one helps the weakest, the poorest. When conversion achieves this, you are sure that it is a true conversion. If you stop at words, it is not a real conversion.

Eucharistic life, prayer, the preaching of the apostles, and the experience of communion (see Acts 2:42) turn believers into a multitude of people who — the Book of the Acts of the Apostles says — are of "one heart and soul" and who do not consider their property their own, but hold everything in common (Acts 4:32). It is such a powerful example of life that it helps us to be generous and not miserly. ...

The Church has always had this gesture of Christians who stripped themselves of the things they had in excess, the things that were not necessary, in order to give them to those in need. And not just money: also time. How many Christians — you for example, here in Italy — how many Christians do volunteer work! This is beautiful. It is communion, sharing one's time with others to help those in need. And thus: Volunteer work, charity work, visits to the sick; we must always share with others and not just seek after our own interests.

In this way, the community, or *koinonia*, becomes the new way of relating among the Lord's disciples. Christians experience a new way of being and behaving among themselves. And it is the proper Christian method, to such an extent that Gentiles would look at Christians and remark, "Look at how they love each other!" Love was the method. But not love in word, not false love: love in works, in helping one another, concrete love, the concreteness of love. The covenant with Christ establishes a bond among brothers and sisters which merges and expresses itself in the communion of material goods, too. Yes, this method of being together, of loving this way, "up to the pocket," also brings one to strip oneself of the hindrance of money and to give it to others, going against one's own interests. Being the limbs of the Body of Christ makes believers share the responsibility for one another. Being believers in Jesus makes us all responsible for each other. "But look at that one, the problem he has. I don't care, it's his business." No, among Christians we cannot [merely] say, "Poor thing, he has a problem at home, he is going through this family problem," but "I have to pray, I take him with me, I am not indifferent." This is being Christian. This is why the strong support the weak (see Rom 15:1) and no one experiences poverty that humiliates and disfigures human dignity because they live in this community: having one heart in common. They love one another. This is the sign: concrete love. ...

Falling short of sincere sharing — indeed, falling short of the sincerity of love — means cultivating hypocrisy, distancing oneself from the truth, becoming selfish, extinguishing the fire of communion and choosing the frost of inner death. ... A life based only on drawing gain and advantages from situations to the detriment of others inevitably causes inner death.

Our being[3] members of one another is the profound motivation with which the apostle exhorts us to put away falsehood and speak the truth. The obligation to safeguard the truth arises from the requirement to not deny our mutual relationship of communion. Truth, in fact, is revealed in communion. Lying, on the other hand, is a selfish refusal to recognize one's belonging to the body. It is a refusal to give oneself to others, thus losing the only way to find oneself.

ALWAYS OPEN TO DIALOGUE
AND ENCOUNTER

Is[4] there something that every one of us, as members of the Holy Mother Church, can and must do? Certainly, there must never be a shortage of prayer, in continuity and in communion with that of Jesus, prayer for the unity of Christians. And together with prayer, the Lord asks us for renewed openness: He asks us not to be closed to dialogue and to encounter, but to welcome all that is valid and positive which is offered even by someone who thinks differently from us or who takes a different stand. He asks us not to fix our gaze on what divides us, but rather on what unites us, seeking to know and love Jesus better and to share the richness of his love. And this means a concrete adherence to the Truth, together with the capacity for reciprocal forgiveness, to feel a part of the same Christian family, to consider oneself a gift for the other, and together to do many good things and works of charity.

WITNESSING TO JESUS CONCERNS
EVERY BAPTIZED PERSON

To[5] feel that we are in communion with the whole Church, with all of the Catholic communities of the world great and small! This is beautiful! And then, to feel we are all on mission, great and small communities alike, that we all must open our doors and go out for the sake of the Gospel. Let us ask ourselves then: What do I do in order to communicate to others the joy of encountering the Lord, the joy of belonging to the Church? Proclaiming and bearing witness to the faith is not the work of the few; it also concerns me, you, each one of us!

ON THE PATH TO UNITY

Meeting[6] each other, seeing each other face to face, exchanging the embrace of peace, and praying for each other, are all essential aspects of our journey toward the restoration of full communion. All of this precedes and always accompanies that other essential aspect of this journey — namely, theological dialogue. An authentic dialogue is, in every case, an encounter between persons with a name, a face, a past, and not merely a meeting of ideas.

In[7] our world, which hungers and thirsts for truth, love, hope, peace and unity, our witness demands that we should at last be able to proclaim with one voice the good news of the Gospel and to celebrate together the divine mysteries of new life in Christ! We are well aware that unity is primarily a gift from God for which we must pray without ceasing, but we all have the task of preparing the conditions, cultivating the ground of our hearts, so that this great grace may be received.

UNIVERSAL BROTHERHOOD

RESPECTING EACH PERSON

What[1] we are called to respect in each person is, first of all, his life, his physical integrity, his dignity and the rights deriving from that dignity, his reputation, his property, his ethnic and cultural identity, his ideas, and his political choices. We are therefore called to think, speak, and write respectfully of the other, not only in his presence, but always and everywhere, avoiding unfair criticism or defamation. Families, schools, religious teaching, and all forms of media have a role to play in achieving this goal.

PEACEFUL COEXISTENCE
BETWEEN RELIGIONS

The[2] peaceful and fruitful coexistence between persons and communities of believers of different religions is not only desirable but possible and realistic. They are putting it into practice! This entails an authentic and fruitful dialogue which spurns relativism and takes the identity of each one into account. What the various religious expressions have in common is, indeed, life's journey, the good will to do good to one's neighbor, without denying or diminishing their respective identity.

The[3] peaceful coexistence of different religious communities is, in fact, an inestimable benefit to peace and to harmonious human advancement. This is something of value which needs to be protected and nourished each day, by providing an education which respects differences and particular identities, so that dialogue and cooperation for the good of all may be promoted and strengthened by mutual understanding and esteem. It is a gift which we need to implore from God in prayer.

We[4] encourage all parties regardless of their religious convictions to continue to work for reconciliation and for the just recognition of peoples' rights. We are persuaded that it is not arms but dialogue, pardon, and reconciliation that are the only possible means to achieve peace.

REBUILDING THROUGH ENCOUNTER

Let[5] everyone be moved to look into the depths of his or her conscience and listen to that word which says: Leave behind the self-interest that hardens your heart, overcome the indifference that makes your heart insensitive toward others, conquer your deadly reasoning, and open yourself to dialogue and reconciliation. Look upon your brother's sorrow —
I think of the children: Look upon these ... look at the sorrow

of your brother, stay your hand and do not add to it, rebuild the harmony that has been shattered — and all this achieved not by conflict but by encounter!

ATTENTION TO VULNERABLE PEOPLE

How[6] important it is that the voice of every member of society be heard, and that a spirit of open communication, dialogue, and cooperation be fostered. It is likewise important that special concern be shown for the poor, the vulnerable, and those who have no voice, not only by meeting their immediate needs, but also by assisting them in their human and cultural advancement.

DIALOGUE

STARTING WITH OUR OWN IDENTITY

Dialogue[1] does not mean renouncing one's own identity when it goes against another's, nor does it mean compromising Christian faith and morals. To the contrary, "true openness involves remaining steadfast in one's deepest convictions, clear and joyful in one's own identity" (*Evangelii Gaudium*, 251) and therefore open to understanding the religions of another, capable of respectful human relationships, convinced that the encounter with someone different than ourselves can be an occasion of growth in a spirit of fraternity, of enrichment, and of witness. This is why interreligious dialogue and evangelization are not mutually exclusive, but rather nourish one another. We do not impose anything [or] do not employ any subtle strategies for attracting believers;

rather, we bear witness to what we believe and who we are with joy and simplicity.

A[2] clear sense of one's own identity and a capacity for empathy are thus the point of departure for all dialogue. If we are to speak freely, openly, and fruitfully with others, we must be clear about who we are, what God has done for us, and what it is that he asks of us. And if our communication is not to be a monologue, there has to be openness of heart and mind to accepting individuals and cultures — fearlessly, for fear is the enemy of this kind of openness.

Dialogue[3] is so important, but to dialogue two things are necessary: one's identity as a starting point and empathy toward others. If I am not sure of my identity and I go to speak, I end up bartering my faith. You cannot dialogue without starting from your own identity and empathy, which is a priori not condemning. Every man, every woman has something of their own to give us; every man, every woman has their own story, their own situation, and we have to listen to it. Then the prudence of the Holy Spirit will tell us how to respond. Start from your own identity in order to dialogue, but a dialogue is not doing apologetics, although sometimes you must do so when ... asked questions that require an explanation. Dialogue is a human thing. It is hearts and souls that dialogue, and this is so important! Do not be afraid to dialogue with anyone.

When[4] a person is secure of his or her own beliefs, there is no need to impose or put pressure on others: There is a conviction that truth has its own power of attraction. Deep down, we are all pilgrims on this earth, and on this pilgrim journey, as we yearn for truth and eternity, we do not live autonomous and self-sufficient individual lives; the same applies to religious, cultural, and national communities. We need each other and are entrusted to each other's care. Each religious tradition, from within, must be able to take account of others. ...

Without identity, there can be no dialogue. It would be an illusory dialogue, a dialogue without substance: It would serve no purpose. All of us have our own religious identity to which we are faithful. But the Lord knows how to guide history. May each one of us begin with our own identity, not pretending to have another, because it serves no end and does not help; it is relativism. What unites us is the path of life, is starting from our own identity for the good of our brothers and sisters. To do good! And so, we walk together as brothers and sisters. Every one of us offers the witness of our identity to others and engages in dialogue with others. Then dialogue can move on to theological questions. But even more important and beautiful is to walk together without betraying our own identity, without disguising it, without hypocrisy. This is what I like to think.

FIRST LISTEN, THEN SPEAK

Dialogue[5] is very important for one's own maturity, because in the comparison with the other person, in the comparison with other cultures, even in the healthy comparison with other religions, we grow: We grow, we mature. ... Listen to others and then speak. First listen, then speak. All this is meekness. And if you don't think like me ... well, you know ... I think differently, you don't convince me — but we're friends anyway. I've heard what you think and you've heard what I think. And you know what, what is important? This dialogue is what makes peace. You can't have peace without dialogue.

THE ONLY PATH TO PEACE

In[6] the world, in society, there is little peace also because dialogue is missing, we find it difficult to go beyond the narrow horizon of our own interests in order to open ourselves to a true and sincere comparison. Peace requires a persistent, patient, strong, intelligent dialogue by which nothing is lost. Dialogue can overcome war. Dialogue can bring people of different generations who often ignore one another to live together; it makes citizens of different ethnic backgrounds and of different beliefs coexist. Dialogue is the way of peace. For dialogue fosters understanding, harmony, concord, and peace. For this reason, it is vital that it grow and expand between people of every condition and belief, like a net of peace that protects the world and especially protects the weakest members.

As religious leaders, we are called to be true "people of dialogue," to cooperate in building peace not as intermediaries but as authentic mediators. Intermediaries seek to give everyone a discount ultimately in order to gain something for themselves. However, the mediator is one who retains nothing for himself, but rather spends himself generously until he is consumed, knowing that the only gain is peace. Each one of us is called to be an artisan of peace, by uniting and not dividing, by extinguishing hatred and not holding on to it, by opening paths to dialogue and not by constructing new walls! Let us dialogue and meet each other in order to establish a culture of dialogue in the world, a culture of encounter.

Between[7] selfish indifference and violent protest there is always another possible option: that of dialogue. Dialogue between generations, dialogue within the people, because we are all that people, the capacity to give and receive, while remaining open to the truth. A country grows when constructive dialogue occurs between its many rich cultural components — popular culture, university culture, youth culture, artistic culture, technological culture, economic culture, family culture, and media culture — when they enter into dialogue.

HUMILITY AND SIMPLICITY

HUMILITY FIRST OF ALL

Dialogue[1] takes place with humility, even at the cost of "swallowing bitter pills," because we must not allow "walls" of resentment and hatred to grow in our hearts. See how David, inspired by the Lord, breaks this mechanism of hatred and says, "No, I want to dialogue with you." This is how the road to peace begins — with dialogue. But dialogue is not easy. It is hard. Yet only "through dialogue are bridges built within relationships and not walls that drive us apart." In order to dialogue, first of all, humility is necessary. And then it is necessary to think that the other person has something more than I do, just as David did when he looked at Saul and said to himself, "He is the Lord's Anointed. He is more important than I am." Along with humility and meekness, to dialogue it is necessary to become all things to all people.

Humility, meekness, and becoming all things to all people are the three basic elements of dialogue. But even if it is not written in the Bible, we all know that to do these things we have to swallow many bitter pills. We must do it because this is how peace is made!

GOODNESS IS CONTAGIOUS

In[2] order to be "imitators of Christ" (see 1 Cor 11:1) in the face of a poor or sick person, we must not be afraid to look him in the eye and to draw near with tenderness and compassion, and to touch him and embrace him. I have often asked this of people who help others, to do so looking them in the eye, not to be afraid to touch them; that this gesture of help may also be a gesture of communication, we too need to be welcomed by them. A gesture of tenderness, a gesture of compassion. ... Let us ask you: When you help others, do you look them in the eye? Do you embrace them without being afraid to touch them? Do you embrace them with tenderness? Think about this: How do you help? From a distance or with tenderness, with closeness? If evil is contagious, so is goodness. Therefore, there needs to be ever more abundant goodness in us. Let us be infected by goodness and let us spread goodness!

ASHAMED OF EVIL

Little ones[3] have a certain wisdom. When a child comes to confession, he or she never says something vague. "Father, I did this, I did this to my aunt, I did this to the other person, to someone else I said this word" ... and they say the word. They are concrete, they have the simplicity of truth.

We [grown-ups] always have the tendency to hide the reality of our wretchedness. Instead, if there is a beautiful thing, it is when, in the presence of God, we confess our sins as they are. May we always feel that grace of shame. To be ashamed before God is a grace. It is a grace — "I am ashamed." To go to confession "is to go to an encounter with the Lord who forgives us, who loves us. And our shame is what we offer to him: 'Lord, I am a sinner, but you see I am not so bad, I am capable of being ashamed.'" Therefore let us ask for ... this grace of living in truth without hiding anything from God and without hiding anything from ourselves.

TRUTH

AUTHENTICITY AND RELATIONSHIP

Freedom[1] from falsehood and the search for relationship: These two ingredients cannot be lacking if our words and gestures are to be true, authentic, and trustworthy. To discern the truth, we need to discern everything that encourages communion and promotes goodness from whatever instead tends to isolate, divide, and oppose. Truth, therefore, is not really grasped when it is imposed from without as something impersonal, but only when it flows from free relationships between persons, from listening to one another. Nor can we ever stop seeking the truth, because falsehood can always creep in, even when we state things that are true. An impeccable argument can indeed rest on undeniable facts, but if it is used to hurt another and to discredit that person in the eyes of others, however correct it may appear, it is not truthful. We can recognize the truth of statements from their fruits: whether they provoke quarrels, foment division, encourage resignation; or, on the other hand, they promote informed and mature reflection leading to constructive dialogue and fruitful results.

Now[2] more than ever, there is a need for news communicated fully, with measured language, so as to encourage reflection — well-considered and clear words, which reject aggressive and scornful tones. Words ... spoken in truth, in goodness, and in beauty.

THE CHURCH, SERVANT OF TRUTH

The[3] first truth of the Church is the love of Christ. The Church is the servant and mediator of this love among people, which reaches even to forgiveness and self-giving. So, wherever the Church is present, the Father's mercy must be evident. In our parishes, communities, associations, and movements — in short, wherever there are Christians — each and every person should be able to find an oasis of mercy.

Christian[4] truth is attractive and persuasive because it responds to the profound need of human life, proclaiming convincingly that Christ is the one Savior of the whole man and of all men. This proclamation remains as valid today as it was at the origin of Christianity, when the first great missionary expansion of the Gospel took place.

GIVING YOUR LIFE

Then[5] there are many people, Christians and non-Christians alike, who "lose their lives" for truth. And Christ said, "I am the truth," therefore whoever serves the truth serves Christ. One of those who gave his life for the truth is John the Baptist: Tomorrow, June 24 is his great feast, the solemnity of his birth. John was chosen by God to prepare the way for Jesus, and he revealed him to the people of Israel as the Messiah, the Lamb of God who takes away the sin of the world (see Jn 1:29). John consecrated himself entirely to God and to his envoy, Jesus. But, in the end, what happened? He died for the sake of the truth when he denounced the adultery of King Herod and Herodias. How many people pay dearly for their commitment to truth! Upright people who are not afraid to go against the current! How many just men prefer to go against the current, so as not to deny the voice of conscience, the voice of truth! And we, we must not be afraid! Among you are many young people. To you, young people, I say: Do not be afraid to go against the current, when they want to rob us of hope, when they propose rotten values, values like food gone bad — and when food has gone bad, it harms us; these values harm us. We must go against the current! And you, young people, are the first: Go against the tide and have the daring to move precisely against the current. Forward, be brave, and go against the tide! And be proud of doing so.

COMMUNICATING WITHIN CULTURE

This[6] is a proposal: a culture of closeness. Isolation and withdrawing into one's own interests are never the way to restore hope and bring about a renewal. Rather, it is closeness, it is the culture of encounter. Isolation, no. Closeness, yes. Culture clash, no; culture of encounter, yes. The university is a privileged place where this culture of dialogue is promoted, taught, and lived, this culture which does not indiscriminately level out differences and plurality — this is one of the risks of globalization — nor does it take them to the extreme, causing them to become causes of conflict. Rather, it opens to constructive dialogue. This means understanding and esteeming someone else's riches; it means not seeing him with indifference or fear, but as an opportunity for growth. The dynamics that regulate relationships between people, groups, and nations often do not involve closeness and encounter, but rather conflict.

CLOSENESS

Communicating[7] well helps bring us together and to know each other better, to be more united. The walls that divide us can only be overcome if we are ready to listen to each other and learn from each other. We need to resolve differences through forms of dialogue that permit us to grow in understanding and respect. The culture of encounter requires us to be willing not only to give, but to receive from others. ... Communication is ultimately more of a human achievement than a technological one. So, what helps us ... to grow in humanity and mutual understanding? We need to recover a certain sense of being unhurried and calm, for example. This requires time and the ability to be quiet so as to listen. We also need to be patient if we want to understand those who are different from us. People express themselves fully not when they are just tolerated, but when they know they are truly embraced. If we are truly willing to listen to others, then we will learn to look at the world with different eyes and to appreciate human experience as it manifests itself in various cultures and traditions. But we will also learn to better appreciate the great values inspired by Christianity, such as the vision of the human being as a person, marriage and the family, the distinction between the religious and political spheres, the principles of solidarity and subsidiarity, and others. ... We have to know how to enter into dialogue with the men and women of today, to understand their expectations, doubts, and hopes, and to offer them the Gospel — that is, Jesus Christ, God made man, who died and rose again to free us from sin and death. The challenge requires depth, attention to life, and spiritual sensitivity. To dialogue means to be convinced that the other person has something good to say, to make room for his or her point of view and proposals. Dialogue does not mean renouncing one's own ideas and traditions, but renouncing the claim that they are singular and absolute.

IN EVERY FIELD OF HUMAN ACTIVITY

The[8] viewing of a cinematographic work can open different chinks of light in the human soul. Everything depends on the emotional charge that is given to the vision. There can be escape, emotion, laughter, anger, fear, interest. ... Everything is connected to the intentionality placed in viewing, which is not just an exercise of the eye, but something more. It is a gaze trained on reality. The gaze, in fact, reveals the most diversified orientation of interiority, because it is capable of seeing things, and seeing inside things. The gaze also provokes consciences to a careful examination. Let us ask ourselves: What is our gaze like? Is it an attentive and close look, not slumbering? Is it an overall gaze, one of unity? In particular, to you who deal with cinema: Is it a look that arouses emotions? Is it a gaze that communicates communion and creativity? The answers are not obvious and require great inner work. The gaze communicates and does not betray, it engages in lifestyles and actions coordinated for a greater good than mere personal interest. The gaze is the foundation of community building. And you know very well how important it is to overcome the barriers of the past to project oneself into the paths of the future. All of you have an ecclesial feeling in your DNA. I urge you to live your passion and your competence with ecclesial sense and style: The best medicine is not to become self-absorbed, which always kills.

A[9] synodal way of proceeding also calls for a journal, which can use its pages to allow positions and points of view to converse; but it must beware of the temptation to be abstract, to limit itself to the level of ideas, forgetting the reality of acting and journeying together. Avoid this risk when publishing words rooted in social experiences and practices, nourished by that reality. Serious intellectual research is also a journey made together, especially when dealing with frontier issues, making different perspectives and disciplines interact, and promoting relationships of respect and friendship between the people involved, who discover how the encounter enriches everyone. This is all the more true in initiatives that require the creation of networks, participation in events, and the activation of research groups. I know that you are involved in many such experiences, some even here in the Vatican, and I encourage you to continue.

Three areas seem to me to be particularly significant. The first is the integration of those parts of society which, for various reasons, are situated on the margins, and in which the victims of the throwaway culture are more easily found.

They are bearers of an original contribution indispensable for the construction of a more just society: They see things that others cannot see.

A second area concerns the encounter between the generations, whose urgency we recognized at the [2018] Synod of Young People. The acceleration of social change risks tearing young people away from their past, projecting them into a future without roots and making them easier to manipulate, while exposing older people to the temptation of imitating youth. To counter these risks, we need to strengthen pacts of trust and solidarity between generations.

Finally, the third area is the promotion of opportunities for encounter and common action between Christians and believers of other religions, but also with all people of goodwill. To do so requires dealing with atavistic fears and very deep-rooted tensions: Some concern interreligious relations, others refer to the clashes between "laity" and "Catholics" that run through Italian history, others — and we must not forget them, indeed they require special attention — are internal to the ecclesial body. But if we do not succeed in uniting the whole human family, it will be impossible to proceed in the search for sustainable and integral development (*Laudato si'*, 13).

Journalists,[10] the guardians of the news ... in today's world, do not just carry out a job, but a real mission. In the frenzy of information and the whirlwind of the news cycle, they have the task of remembering that the center of the news is not the speed of its delivery or its impact on the audience, but real people. To inform is to educate, to engage with people's lives.

Each[11] new drama that happens in world history also be-

comes the possible scenario of good news, since love always
manages to find the path of proximity and to arouse hearts
capable of being moved, faces able to stay positive, hands
ready to build.

YOUNG PEOPLE

GROWING IN THE CULTURE OF ENCOUNTER

Building[1] walls is not helpful. A short time ago I quoted that beautiful phrase of Ivo Andric in the novel "The Bridge on the Drina," when he speaks of bridges and says that bridges are something so indescribable and so great that they are angels, they are not human things. He says this: "The bridge was made by God from angels' wings so that men can communicate." The greatness of building bridges with people is for communication, and we grow with communication. Closing off within ourselves leads us to be noncommunicators, to be "distilled water," without strength. This is why I tell you: "Teach young people, help young people to grow in culture and in encounter, to be capable of encountering different people, differences, and to grow with differences: This is how we grow, with comparison, with good comparison."

The[2] university is a privileged place where this culture of dialogue is promoted, taught, and lived, this culture which does not indiscriminately level out differences and plurality — this is one of the risks of globalization — nor does it take them to the extreme, causing them to become causes of conflict. Rather, it opens to constructive dialogue. This means understanding and esteeming someone else's riches; it means not seeing him with indifference or fear, but as an opportunity for growth. The dynamics that regulate relationships between people, groups, and nations often do not involve closeness and encounter, but rather conflict.

My[3] hope is that, more than a celebration of sport, [the 2014] World Cup can be a celebration of solidarity among nations. This, however, presupposes that the football matches should be considered as what they really are: a game and, at the same time, an opportunity for dialogue, understanding, and mutual enrichment of the human person. Sport is not only a form of entertainment, but also — and I would say above all — a tool to communicate values which promote the good of the human person and contribute to building a more peaceful and fraternal society. Just think of loyalty, perseverance, friendship, sharing, solidarity. There are, in fact, many values and attitudes which football promotes, and which prove to be important not only on the field but in all fields of existence, and specifically in building peace. Sport is a school of peace; it teaches us how to build peace.

In[4] studying and in the forms of digital communication your friends sometimes experience loneliness, a lack of hope and faith in their own abilities. Bring hope and always show your work to others, always be open to sharing, to dialogue. Especially in today's culture we need to place ourselves at everyone's side. You can overcome conflict between peoples only if you manage to nurture a culture of encounter and of fraternity. I exhort you to continue to bring the Gospel into the university and culture into the Church!

TRANSFORMING THE WORLD

Let[5] us think of the meaning of that multitude of young people who encountered the Risen Christ in Rio de Janeiro and who bring his love to everyday life, who live it and communicate it. They are not going to end up in the newspapers because they don't perpetrate acts of violence; they don't give rise to scandal, and so they don't make news. Yet if they stay united to Jesus, they build his kingdom, they build brotherhood, sharing, works of mercy, they are a powerful force to make the world more just and more beautiful, to transform it!

In[6] my meetings with political leaders from various European countries, I have observed that the younger politicians view reality differently than their older colleagues. They may appear to be saying the same things, but their approach is different. The lyrics are the same, but the music is different. This is evident in younger politicians from various parties. This empirical fact points to a reality of present-day Europe which cannot be overlooked in efforts to unite the Continent and to guide its future: We need to take into account this transversality encountered in every sector. To do so requires engaging in dialogue, including intergenerational dialogue. Were we to define the Continent today, we should speak of a Europe in dialogue, one which puts a transversality of opinions and reflections at the service of a harmonious union of peoples.

INTERNET AND SOCIAL MEDIA

The digital environment[7] is a characteristic of the contemporary world. Broad swathes of humanity are immersed in it in an ordinary and continuous manner. It
is no longer merely a question of 'using' instruments
of communication, but of living in a highly digitalized
culture that has had a profound impact on ideas of
time and space, on our self-understanding, our understanding of others and the world, and our ability
to communicate, learn, be informed, and enter into
relationship with others. An approach to reality that
privileges images over listening and reading has in-
fluenced the way people learn and the development of
their critical sense." (*Christus Vivit*, 86)

The new culture, marked by the factors of convergence
and multimedia, needs a suitable response from the Apostolic See in the area of communication. Today, with respect to a
diversified array of services, multimedia prevails, and it also
marks out the way they are conceived, thought out, and im-
plemented. All this implies, along with cultural change, an
institutional and personal conversion, from working in silos
— which in the best cases had some coordination — to working in an intrinsically connected way, in synergy. ... All this
has particular value in our time, because what we are living
through *is not simply an era of change, but a change of era.*
We are, therefore, in one of those moments in which chang-

es are no longer linear, but epochal. They constitute choices that rapidly transform our way of living, of relating, of communicating and elaborating thought, of relating between human generations, and of understanding and living faith and science. It often happens that we experience change merely by changing clothes, and then actually remaining as we were before. I recall the enigmatic expression in a famous Italian novel *Il Gattopardo* by Giuseppe Tomasi di Lampedusa: "If we want everything to remain the same, everything must change." A healthy attitude, instead, means to let oneself be questioned by the challenges of the present time and to face them through the virtues of discernment, *parresia,* and *hypomoné.* In such a case, change takes on an entirely different aspect. Instead of an element of surroundings, context or pretext, an external landscape ... it would become increasingly human, and even more Christian. It would still mean an external change, but it would start at the very center of the human being — that is, an anthropological conversion.

A GREAT OPPORTUNITY

How[8] I would like the media to pay more attention to young people, not only by telling of their failures, but also their dreams and their hopes! The gospel of joy calls us to an educational commitment that can no longer be postponed. Educating young people in the school of the Gospel means, above all, being witnesses of the only Word that saves. May your communication be outbound, to engage in dialogue and, first and foremost, to listen to young people. Let us remember: The Gospel asks to dare!

Communication,[9] wherever and however it takes place,

has opened up broader horizons for many people. This is a gift of God which involves a great responsibility. I like to refer to this power of communication as "closeness." The encounter between communication and mercy will be fruitful to the degree that it generates a closeness which cares, comforts, heals, accompanies, and celebrates. In a broken, fragmented, and polarized world, to communicate with mercy means to help create a healthy, free, and fraternal closeness between the children of God and all our brothers and sisters in the one human family.

... NOT WITHOUT RISKS

The internet[10] and social media are a resource for our time. They are an opportunity to keep in touch with others, to share values and plans, and to express a desire to form community. The web can also help us to pray in community, to pray together. The media sometimes present the family as if it were an abstract model to accept or reject, defend or attack, instead of a concrete reality to be lived. Or [they present it] as if it were an ideology of someone against someone else, instead of the place where we all learn what it means to communicate in love received and given. On the contrary, telling stories means understanding that our lives are woven together, that there are many voices and each one is irreplaceable.

Being[11] people of hope means finding the courage to face some of today's challenges. I am thinking, for example, of the responsible use of the media. They convey positive news, but they can also destroy the dignity of persons, weaken spiritual momentum, and harm fraternal life. We must educate ourselves to use these media in an evangelical way.

FAMILY

UNION WITH GOD AND OUR LOVED ONES

[In the family we realize that others have preceded us. This] experience[1] ... enables the family to become the setting in which the most basic form of communication, which is prayer, is handed down. When parents put their newborn children to sleep, they frequently entrust them to God, asking that he watch over them. When the children are a little older, parents help them to recite some simple prayers, thinking with affection of other people, such as grandparents, relatives, the sick and suffering, and all those in need of God's help. It was in our families that the majority of us learned the religious dimension of communication, which in the case of Christianity is permeated with love, the love that God bestows upon us and which we then offer to others.

If[2] the door of the family is not open to the presence of God and to his love, then the family loses its harmony, individualism prevails, and joy is extinguished. Instead, the family which experiences joy — the joy of life, the joy of faith — communicates it spontaneously, is the salt of the earth, and light of the world, the leaven for all of society.

THE SCHOOL OF RELATIONSHIPS

How[3] important grandparents are for family life, for passing on the human and religious heritage which is so essential for each and every society. How important it is to have intergenerational exchanges and dialogue, especially within the context of the family. ... This relationship and this dialogue between generations is a treasure to be preserved and strengthened!

Our[4] personality develops in the family, by growing up with our mom and dad, our brothers and sisters, by breathing in the warmth of the home. The family is the place where we receive our name, it is the place of affection, the space of intimacy, where one acquires the art of dialogue and interpersonal communication. ... The "good news" of the family is a very important part of evangelization, which Christians can communicate to all, by the witness of their lives; and already they are doing so ... evident in secularized societies. Truly Christian families are known by their fidelity, their patience, their openness to life, and by their respect for the elderly. ... The secret to this is the presence of Jesus in the family.

It's[5] good for the elderly to communicate their wisdom to the young; and it's good for the young people to gather this wealth of experience and wisdom, and to carry it forward, not so as to safeguard it in a museum, but to carry it forward addressing the challenges that life brings, to carry it forward for the sake of the respective religious orders and of the whole Church.

WITH THE LOOK OF JESUS*

*And as he was setting out on his journey, a man ran up
and knelt before him, and asked him, "Good Teacher,
what must I do to inherit eternal life?" And Jesus said
to him, "Why do you call me good? No one is good but
God alone. You know the commandments: 'Do not
kill, do not commit adultery, do not steal, do not bear
false witness, do not defraud, honor your father and
mother.'" And he said to him, "Teacher, all these I have
observed from my youth." And Jesus looking upon him
loved him, and said to him, "You lack one thing; go,
sell what you have, and give to the poor, and you will
have treasure in heaven; and come, follow me." At
that saying his countenance fell, and he went away*

*An unpublished text of Pope Francis

sorrowful; for he had great possessions.
   *And Jesus looked around and said to his disciples,
"How hard it will be for those who have riches to enter
the kingdom of God!" And the disciples were amazed
at his words. But Jesus said to them again, "Children,
how hard it is for those who trust in riches to enter the
kingdom of God! It is easier for a camel to go through
the eye of a needle than for a rich man to enter the
kingdom of God." And they were exceedingly aston-
ished, and said to him, "Then who can be saved?" Jesus looked at them and said, "With men it is impossible, but not with God; for all things are possible with
God."*

Mark 10:17–27

All three synoptic Gospels report the episode of the "rich
young man," of that man — we actually can't deduce his exact
age from the texts — who asks Jesus what he must do to inherit eternal life. In this brief dialogue there is a detail that only
the Gospel of Mark reports, in the middle of the conversation,
between a question and an answer. The evangelist writes that
"Jesus looking upon him loved him" (Mk 10:21). This detail
seems decisive to me. It is a detail that says a lot about the
style of Jesus, about that style which is "essence" and "substance" and shows us a truly human way to live in the world.
To be human means to communicate, to get in touch with the
world and with others, and to build relationships.

   While the two are talking, Jesus is not only thinking
about what he wants to say to his interlocutor, but he is
thinking about him, about who is in front of him. Even be-

fore thinking, he looks at him, sets his gaze on him with love. Jesus showed this style not only with the rich young man, but with all the people he met. After all, the Gospel is — also — the story of the many encounters of Jesus along his path through the streets of Palestine. In some cases it is easy to imagine that this "looking upon him [Jesus] loved him" happened, even if not stated explicitly in Jesus' other encounters. Think of the call of Matthew (looked upon with mercy and chosen at the same time), the nocturnal dialogue with Nicodemus, or the [encounter] at Jacob's well with the Samaritan woman, and perhaps even the more brief ones with the Canaanite woman and Zacchaeus. Surely that look is the same one with which Jesus offers his cheek to Judas calling him "friend," the same look with which he turns to Peter as the cock crows, and, even if we find it hard to understand, the same look with which he silently observes the wretched spectacle of King Herod expecting some miraculous gesture before disappointedly sending Jesus back to Pilate. Even in the dialogue with the Roman procurator, Jesus would have looked at him with love.

The Christian faith is founded on this simple affirmation: Jesus is divine in nature and God is love. This foundation dictates a series of consequences and changes the Christian's entire way of being in the world. Without this look of love, human communication, the dialogue between people, can easily become just a dialectical duel. That look reveals instead that there is another issue at stake, something dizzying, which does not have at its center the merit of the discussion, but much more, the very meaning of existence, both mine and that of the other person.

The evangelist uses an interesting term: "looking upon," a verb that implies a contemplative attitude, which in turn requires an extended time, a stopping of the moment almost to savor each instant. In Western societies in particular the verb "to look upon," the contemplative attitude, seems to have had its citizenship revoked. It seems to have disappeared from the daily landscape, from everyday life. No one looks at anyone else, and if it happens, it automatically triggers unease and a reaction as if to a danger. Something has been lost: No one looks into each other's eyes, no one "stops" in front of the other to momentarily pause the frantic race of time that rules over us. With this condition in mind, on my return from my trip to Asia last November I expressed the hope that the West would recover from the East the sense of "poetry." With this beautiful word I meant the sense of contemplation, of stopping and granting a moment of openness toward oneself and others in a sign of gratuitousness, of pure selflessness. Without that "more" of poetry, without this gift, without gratuitousness, there can be no true encounter, nor a truly human communication. People "communicate" not only by exchanging information, but by trying to build communion. Words must therefore be like bridges for bringing different positions closer, creating common ground, a place of encounter, comparison, and growth.

The basic condition for this *rapprochement* is being willing to patiently listen to the positions of the other. Looking upon someone presupposes accepting to be looked upon. In communication one offers oneself to the other.

On this subject there is much to learn from the teaching of the sainted Cardinal John Henry Newman. His reflections focused particularly on the dimension of imagination and the "dispositions" of the heart, which play a more important role than that of reason, for a person to truly be touched by the experience of faith. Newman realized that people often argued and ended up quarreling not because of the merits of the discussion, but because of a predisposition of greater or lesser openness toward each other. His was not an abstract reflection, but one that started from the experience of constant dialogue with his younger brother, Charles, who had become an atheist. "You are not in the frame of mind of someone willing to listen to arguments, whatever they may be," he wrote to his brother who, according to him, ends up falling into disbelief because of an "inadequacy of the heart, not of the intellect," because when it comes to religious matters people tend to see everything "through the lens of prior habits." What was true of his brother Charles is true of today's society, in which it is difficult to find an atheism that comes from a state of open hostility to the Gospel. Instead, it is easy to find an indifference stemming from a series of prejudices and an imagination that stays at a superficial level and does not allow itself to be affected by the disruptive power of Christianity's symbols and messages. If personal disposition is fundamental, then what is needed on every occasion of communication is to try and live it as a true encounter, not a superficial one, open to a fruitful, generative dialogue that sets in motion a dynamism that can disrupt and transform "predispositions." In other words, open to conversion.

It takes courage. As I said on February 4, 2019, in the interreligious meeting at the Founder's Memorial in Abu Dhabi, effective dialogue presupposes having one's own identity, not to be foregone to please the other person. But at the same time it demands the courage of otherness, which involves the full recognition of the other and his or her freedom. ... Without freedom we are no longer children of the human family but slaves. ... The courage of otherness is the heart of dialogue, which is based on sincerity of intentions. ... In all this, prayer is essential: While sincerely intended prayer incarnates the courage of otherness in regard to God, it also purifies the heart from turning in on itself.[1]

Identity and otherness exist together and can only coexist in a context of courage, freedom, and prayer. Otherness is vital to identity. *Never Without the Other*, the title of a beautiful book by Michel De Certeau, is a wonderful motto that can highlight how human existence finds its fullness and ultimate meaning in relationship. A heart turned in on itself becomes sick and "encrusted" with waste that prevents a healthy and life-giving pulse. The relationship has its own breath that needs a rhythm and healthy oxygen, conditions assured only by the presence of the other. My identity is a starting point, but without otherness it falls flat, withers, and risks dying. Without the recognition of otherness, not only the other, but I also, die. The important thing, however, is that this recognition, in order to be full, must be open to recognize the other's freedom. This point is crucial.

Here we move anew into the heart of Christianity. Once again, the Gospel text from which we began comes to the rescue, this time with the second term contained in that phrase:

"Jesus looking upon him loved him." Jesus does not look at the other person as a "spectacle," but as a person, as a gift, as a being that God willed to create freely (out of love) and put on his path. His look of love already includes the dimension of freedom. We love only in freedom, and only true love makes others free. From this standpoint, the way Mark's episode ends is illuminating. We could say that the ending is bitter, that it "ends badly." The young man is disappointed, disconcerted and goes away "sorrowful." The evangelist also explains the reason for this attitude ("he had great possessions"), which could also be translated as, "Because he was not a free person." As if possessions prevented the good. A polytheistic life stifles the possibility of a full, "eternal" life, as the young man asks, and it is not by chance that he lists all the commandments of the law that he keeps without giving him the happiness his heart thirsts for.

Freedom is the crux of this existential situation. Those numerous goods do not allow access to true freedom. Freedom is the essential seasoning for making people's existence on earth fully human, and therefore also every act of communication fully human. Without freedom there is no truth. Every relationship becomes fiction, hypocrisy, slides into superficiality or, worse, into instrumentalization. I approach [others] to use them and thus end up taking away their freedom. Instead, it is strictly a relationship based on love that guarantees my own freedom and that of others, even if this means exposing myself to risk.

To love means to be open to risk. Jesus, in the moment in which he looks on the young man in front of him, does not "size him up" in order to find his weaknesses, but contemplates him, as if he had just come out of the creative hands of God the Father and is happy with his existence. He loves him and calls him to overcome all his prisons and past wounds for a future of fullness, thus answering his question about the possibility of eternal life. In this gesture Jesus exposes himself to risk, he bets on the other, on a human being, and as such the possibility of failure is real. In fact, the episode seems to close in a disastrous way. The word of Jesus, the Word of God, had no effect. The communication between the two, seen as a dialectical skirmish, did not produce any fruit: both "lost." It is the "drama of freedom," as Dostoevsky would say. But this is not the end, as we can see from Jesus' subsequent words. This drama can be overcome by the gesture of prayer, of openness to the otherness of God for whom "nothing is impossible." And it is interesting that Jesus makes this solemn affirmation, once again, and "looks at him."

May God's look always rest on our lives, and may we, in turn, as we enter into relationship and communicate with others, have the same look as Jesus, who looks on us with the eyes of gratuitous and generous love to the point of total self-giving.

NOTES

Some Words about Relationships

1. Message for the LIII World Communications Day. "We are members one of another (Eph 4:25). From social network communities to the human community," January 24, 2019.

2. Angelus, February 1, 2015.

3. Daily meditation in the *Domus Sanctae Marthae*, June 3, 2013.

4. To the presidents of the Bishops' Conference of the Netherlands on an *ad limina Apostolorum* visit, December 2, 2013.

5. Daily meditation in the *Domus Sanctae Marthae*, September 26, 2013.

6. To the participants of the Plenary Session of the Congregation for the Oriental Churches, November 21, 2013.

7. Vigil of Pentecost with the Ecclesial Movements, May 18, 2013.

8. Angelus, August 9, 2015.

9. Angelus, November 10, 2019.

10. General Audience, June 19, 2019.

11. Divine Liturgy in St. George's Patriarchal Church, Istanbul, November 30, 2014.

12. To the community of writers of *La Civiltà Cattolica*, June 14, 2013.

13. Angelus, December 29, 2019.

14. To the students at the School of Journalism from Germany, November 9, 2018.

Our Faith in the God of Relationships
1. Angelus, May 31, 2015.
2. To the Dicastery for Communication of the Holy See, September 23, 2019.
3. Homily for the Solemnity of the Most Holy Body and Blood of Christ, June 19, 2014.
4. Angelus, July 26, 2015.
5. *Lectio divina* at the Pontifical Lateran University, March 26, 2019.
6. Angelus, January 25, 2015.
7. Angelus, July 19, 2015.
8. Homily at Assisi, October 4, 2013.
9. To participants in the "I Can" World Meeting, November 30, 2019.
10. Letter to Eugenio Scalfari, November 10, 2013.
11. General Audience, May 15, 2013.
12. General Audience, November 14, 2018.
13. Regina Coeli, May 24, 2015.
14. Angelus, August 9, 2015.
15. *Lumen Fidei*, June 29, 2013, 40.
16. Ibid., 32.

Daily ... Together
1. December 17, 2014.
2. January 7, 2015.
3. January 28, 2015.
4. February 4, 2015.
5. February 11, 2015.
6. February 18, 2015.
7. March 11, 2015.
8. March 18, 2015.
9. April 15, 2015.
10. April 22, 2015.
11. May 13, 2015.
12. June 3, 2015.
13. June 10, 2015.
14. June 17, 2015.
15. Benedict XVI, Angelus, November 2, 2008.
16. June 24, 2015.

Enemies of Unity
1. General Audience, November 14, 2018.
2. Message for the LII World Communications Day. "'The truth will make you free' (Jn 8:32): Fake News and Peace Journalism," January 24, 2018.
3. To the managers and staff of Telepace, December 13, 2018.
4. Homily at the Catholic Cathedral of the Holy Spirit, Istanbul, November 29, 2014.

5. Daily meditation at the *Domus Sanctae Marthae*, January 24, 2014.
6. Angelus, September 1, 2019.
7. *Vultum Dei quaerere*, June 29, 2016.
8. Regina Coeli, April 19, 2015.
9. To participants at the International Conference on Human Trafficking organized by the Migrants and Refugees Section of the Dicastery for the Service of Integral Human Development, April 11, 2019.
10. *Laudato Si'*, May 24, 2015.
11. Meeting with the students of the "Visconti" High School in Rome on the occasion of the Aloisians' Jubilee Year, April 13, 2019.
12. To the participants of the Fourth World Day of Prayer and Reflection against Trafficking in Persons, February 12, 2018.
13. Letter to the archbishop of Milan on the occasion of the XCIV National Day for the Sacred Heart Catholic University, April 15, 2018.
14. *Lumen Fidei*, 27, June 29, 2013.
15. Ibid., 34.
16. Press conference during the return flight from the apostolic journey to Mozambique, Madagascar, and Mauritius, September 10, 2019.

Journeying in Faith and Mutual Love

1. General Audience, November 6, 2013.
2. Message for the XLVIII World Communications Day. "Communication at the Service of an Authentic Culture of Encounter," January 24, 2014.
3. Benedict XVI, Message for the 47th World Communications Day, 2013.
4. Regina Coeli, April 6, 2015.
5. At the plenary of the Pontifical Council for the Laity, December 7, 2013.
6. Daily meditation at the *Domus Sanctae Marthae*, December 12, 2013.
7. Angelus, March 22, 2015.
8. Message for L World Day of Social Communications. "Communication and Mercy: A Fruitful Encounter," January 24, 2016.
9. To the participants in the plenary assembly of the Dicastery for Communication of the Holy See, September 23, 2019.
10. Angelus, August 18, 2013.
11. To the participants of the International Congress on Catechesis, September 27, 2013.
12. Angelus, February 1, 2015.
13. To the managers and staff of the newspaper *Avvenire*, May 1, 2018.
14. Paul VI, Address to Social Communications Workers, November 27, 1971.

Ecclesial Communion

1. Regina Coeli, May 19, 2019.

2. General Audience, August 21, 2019.
3. Message for the LIII World Communications Day. "'We are all members of one body' (Eph 4:25): From Social Network Communities to Human Community," January 24, 2019.
4. General Audience, October 8, 2014.
5. General Audience, October 9, 2013.
6. Divine Liturgy in St. George's Patriarchal Church, Istanbul, November 30, 2014.
7. To the delegation of the Ecumenical Patriarchate of Constantinople, June 28, 2013.

Universal Brotherhood
1. Message to Muslims worldwide at the end of Ramadan, July 10, 2013.
2. General Audience, September 24, 2014.
3. Meeting with civil authorities, Tirana, Albania, September 21, 2014.
4. Joint statement between Pope Francis and Ecumenical Patriarch Bartholomew I, Jerusalem, May 25, 2014.
5. Prayer Vigil for Peace, September 7, 2013.
6. Meeting with authorities (on the occasion of the Sixth Asian Youth Day), Seoul, August 14, 2014.

Dialogue
1. At the plenary of the Pontifical Council for Interreligious Dialogue, November 28, 2013.
2. Meeting with the bishops of Asia at the shrine of Haemi (South Korea), August 17, 2014.
3. Meeting with diocesan priests, Caserta, Italy, July 26, 2014.
4. Meeting with leaders of other religions and other Christian denominations, Tirana, Albania, September 21, 2014.
5. To the students and teachers of Seibu Gakuen Bunri Junior High School in Saitama, Tokyo, August 21, 2013.
6. At the International Meeting for Peace sponsored by the Community of Sant'Egidio, September 30, 2013.
7. Meeting with Brazil's ruling class, Rio de Janeiro, July 27, 2013.

Humility and Simplicity
1. Daily meditation at the *Domus Sanctae Marthae*, January 24, 2014.
2. Angelus, February 15, 2015.
3. Daily meditation at the *Domus Sanctae Marthae*, October 25, 2013.

Truth
1. Message for the 52nd World Communications Day. " 'The truth will make you free'

(Jn 8:32): Fake News and Peace Journalism," January 24, 2018.

2. To the delegation of the RAI regional media, September 16, 2019.

3. *Misericordiae Vultus*, April 11, 2015.

4. Audience with the College of Cardinals, March 15, 2013.

5. Angelus, June 23, 2013.

6. Meeting with the academic and cultural world, pastoral visit to Cagliari, Italy, September 22, 2013.

7. Message for 48th Social Communications Day, January 24, 2014.

8. Greeting representatives of the Catholic Association of Cinema Exhibitors (ACE-C)-Community Halls (CSE) on the occasion of the 70th anniversary of the community, December 7, 2019.

9. Meeting with the editors and contributors of the journal *Aggiornamenti Sociali*, December 6, 2019.

10. Message for the 52nd Social Communications Day. "'The truth will make you free' (Jn 8:32): Fake News and Peace Journalism," January 24, 2018.

11. Message for the 51st World Communications Day. "'Fear not, for I am with you' (Is 43:5): Communicating Hope and Trust in Our Time,'" January 24, 2017.

Young People

1. Meeting with faculty and students at Collegio San Carlo, Milan, April 6, 2019.

2. At the meeting with the world of culture in the lecture hall of the Pontifical Theological Faculty of Sardinia, Cagliari, Italy, September 22, 2013.

3. Video message on the occasion of the opening of the World Cup, June 12, 2014.

4. Message to the Italian Catholic University Federation (FUCI), October 14, 2014.

5. General Audience, September 4, 2013.

6. To the Council of Europe, Strasbourg, France, November 25, 2014.

7. Christmas greetings to the Roman Curia, December 21, 2019.

8. To the managers and staff of Telepace, December 13, 2018.

9. Message for 50th World Communications Day. "Communication and Mercy: A Fruitful Encounter," January 24, 2016.

10. Angelus, January 20, 2019.

11. Meeting with participants in the General Chapter of the Order of Servants of Mary, October 25, 2019.

Family

1. Message for the XLIX World Communications Day, "Communicating the Family: A Privileged Place of Encounter with the Gift of Love," January 23, 2015.

2. Angelus, December 27, 2015.

3. Angelus, July 26, 2013.

4. To the participants in the plenary assembly of the Pontifical Council for the Family, October 25, 2013.

5. Homily for the feast of the Presentation of the Lord, February 2, 2014.

With the Look of Jesus

1. Interreligious meeting address of Pope Francis, Founder's Memorial (Abu Dhabi), February 4, 2019.

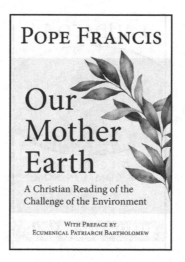

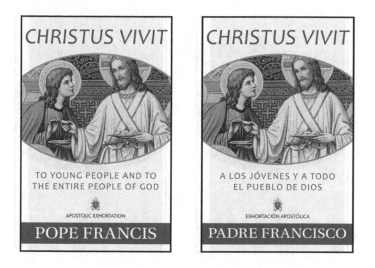

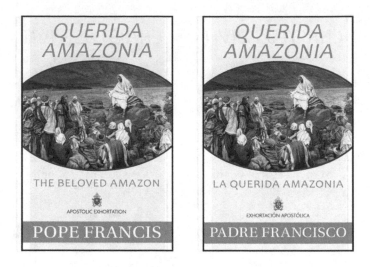

In this apostolic exhortation, *Querida Amazonia* ("The Beloved Amazon"), Pope Francis offers a response to the Synod of Bishops for the Amazon held in Rome in October 2019 and its final document *The Amazon: New Paths for the Church and for an Integral Ecology.*

The pope writes this exhortation to all the faithful calling us to the task of addressing the serious social, environmental, and spiritual issues facing the region. Pope Francis asks: "How can we not struggle together? How can we not pray and work together, side by side, to defend the poor of the Amazon region, to show the sacred countenance of the Lord, and to care for his work of creation?"